Targeted as a Spy:

The Surveillance of an American Diplomat in Communist Romania

Ernest H. Latham, Jr.

Targeted as a Spy:

The Surveillance of an American Diplomat in Communist Romania

Edited by Dennis Deletant and Vadim Guzun

VITA HISTRIA

Vita Histria

Las Vegas ◊ Chicago ◊ Palm Beach

Published in the United States of America by
Histria Books
7181 N. Hualapai Way, Suite 130-86
Las Vegas, NV 89166 USA
HistriaBooks.com

Vita Histria is an imprint of Histria Books. Titles published under the imprints of Histria Books are distributed worldwide.

Library of Congress Control Number: 2020947616

ISBN 978-1-59211-063-6 (hardcover)
ISBN 978-1-59211-195-4 (softbound)
ISBN 978-1-59211-256-2 (eBook)

Contents

Introduction

This book has its origins long after the December 1989 Revolution in Romania. It was only after much debate and discussion that the Romanian Government finally decided to release the files of the secret police, the despised and feared Securitate. I was delighted to learn that I could join the considerable line waiting to see the files and ultimately satisfy a two-decade curiosity as to what that shadowy presence in my life had really intended and what they really thought about me and my activities. As the Scottish poet Bobby Burns had written in his poem *To a Louse*: "O wad some Pow'r the giftie gie us/To see oursels as others see us!" This was my opportunity, a rare one in life, to see myself and learn from an uncensored and unabridged text exactly what some observant and presumably intelligent as well as hostile people saw when they looked at me.

When after a long wait I was told my file was available, as quickly as possible I went to the C.N.S.A.S. headquarters, paid the modest fee and looked forward to the pleasure of soon having some of my long-standing questions answered. What I had not expected was the elephantine size of the file I would have to wade through in pursuit of those answers. In all it came to five volumes, around 2500 documents and, as many were written on both sides of the paper, well over 3000 pages. Obviously, it would require time and a concentrated effort to make a coherent whole out of such a mass of miscellaneous reports, and I procrastinated about making such a focused effort.

A solution to my procrastination came at a meeting with the Romanian diplomat and historian, Dr. Vadim Guzun, in May of 2017. We had first met around 2011 when he published a collection of documents from the Romanian diplomatic archives, *Foametea, piatiletka și ferma colectivă, 1926-1936*, and I had reviewed it favorably in *Holodomor Studies* (Vol. 3, Nos. 1-2). In the years since, we have stayed in touch and he has continued to collect and publish important documents from Central and Eastern Europe in the fields of diplomacy, intelligence, and secret police activities. On one occasion, I happened to mention my unutilized Securitate file, and he asked me if he could see it. That evening I sent him an e-mail with the first of the five volumes. Shortly thereafter he got back in touch saying, "I think we may have a book here." Thus encouraged, I e-mailed the other volumes and, pressured by my imminent departure for Washington, I set up an immediate meeting to discuss the project. Initially we agreed to jointly edit the prospective book.

On second thought, I reneged on such an arrangement. Upon further reflection, I decided that Dr. Guzun had far more experience in such documents than I had. He would inevitably have to be the upper hand in our project. Furthermore, I feared if my name appeared as co-editor on the title page, it would imply I had had an equal role in determining which documents to include and exclude. There would always be a suspicion that the selection reflected my personal wishes, and in the end it would detract from the scholarly worth of the finished project.

The one exception to this resolution is the document #55, which already appeared in the Romanian edition and I expressly asked to be included in this English edition. It is a report by some Securitate source "Stan" on June 27, 1987, towards the end of my tour in Romania. "Stan" is reporting on a conversation with my driver of four years, Ionel Ripeanu. According to "Stan", Ripeanu reported to him that I had been "C.I.A. chief for all N.A.T.O. troops in Europe" and "his appointment to

Romania was a sort of vacation." Even assuming that such a position exists in the CIA, which I doubt, it most assuredly would not have been in neutral Vienna, Austria, or in the American Sector of Berlin, miles behind the Iron Curtain, the only posts in Western Europe that I had held before that time. Furthermore, Ripeanu had been my driver over the previous four years. He would have seen the work I had been doing from early in the morning to late at night, frequently reaching into weekends. He knew very well that this was no vacation by any common definition of the word. Assuming that "Stan" was not making up completely a conversation with Ripeanu, one wonders what Ripeanu thought he was doing with such foolish claims. Was he simply pulling "Stan's" leg, or was he enhancing his own importance as the driver and associate of such an important and dangerous person? I wanted the document included because it well illustrates in a concentrated form just how silly and speculative as such files are.

The formula we finally settled on was that I would write an introduction providing background on myself, my career, my activities in Romania, and my feelings about the files at that time and since. The result is the introduction that you are now reading.

Romania played only a limited role in my youth. I was an avid stamp collector, and I suppose there must have been some Romanian stamps in my collection. I'm sure I could have found Romania on a Mercator projection map. For the rest, Romania was another of the states of Central and Eastern Europe that had fallen under the control of the Soviet Union that were collectively known as the Soviet satellites. It was one of those countries united under a communist tyranny, bound together by the Warsaw Pact, the economic ambitions of COMECON, and a rigid hostility to the Western democracies and the freedoms we believed we represented. That was my impression, reinforced by the Berlin Blockade and the Hungarian Revolution of 1956, not to mention my four years in uniform as a naval officer in the United States Coast Guard and continuous service thereafter in the reserves.

I joined the American Foreign Service in 1966, serving initially as an Arabist in Lebanon and Saudi Arabia. When a number of Arab League countries broke diplomatic relations with the United States in the wake of the June War of 1967, there were few positions left for the junior officers. My record indicated that I spoke German, and I was posted to Vienna in support of the SALT I talks, jokingly remembered as the salt that did not lose its savor. Thus, I restarted my career as a Cold Warrior. From Vienna, I was sent back to Washington for Greek language training in preparation for an assignment in public diplomacy and later as the supervisory political officer at the American Embassy in Nicosia, Cyprus.

It is in Nicosia that my involvement with Romania really begins. It was there in the lobby of the American Embassy, sometime in the mid-1970s, that I picked up by chance off a coffee table a magazine with a photo essay on the painted churches of Bucovina. I was fascinated by the subject. Having been raised in a mill town on the Merrimack River in Massachusetts with a large Greek immigrant population served by three Greek Orthodox churches and currently living in Cyprus, I was familiar with the Orthodox tradition of mural painting *inside* churches. These paintings, however, were on the *outside* of the churches, more naïve in their execution, and certainly more dramatic in their subject matter, for example the Last Judgment with some souls ascending into Heaven and others being pitch-forked down into Hell or set piece battles before the walls of Constantinople. I resolved then and there I would someday see for myself these marvelous churches, an unlikely resolve for an American diplomat in the midst of the Cold War.

In 1977, in keeping with my newly minted persona as a Cold Warrior, I was posted to the American Military Government in the American

Sector of Berlin. The following year I met an American teacher there, and we were married in the summer of 1979. My wife had been living in Europe for several years, and I had been in and out of most European countries. In short, if we wanted to have our honeymoon in a European place completely new for both of us, there were only two possible countries, Albania and Romania. As Enver Hoxha's Albania was completely out of the question for an American diplomat, even if I could have gotten a visa as I most assuredly could not have. That left Romania, and thus it was in October of that year we flew out of Schoenefeld Flughafen in East Berlin to Otopeni Airport in Bucharest. The centerpiece of the next two weeks was a flight to Suceava, where we rented a car and visited the long awaited, much anticipated painted churches. Their vivid colors and painstaking designs captivated me, and their impact has not diminished after many subsequent visits. They will always be one of the few things in my life that truly exceeded my expectations.

From Berlin, I was posted back to Washington, and I was working as Special Assistant to the director of the United States Information Agency in the fall of 1982 when the position of cultural attaché in our embassy in Bucharest suddenly and unexpectedly became vacant. I was asked if I would allow my name to go forward for the assignment. Without hesitation, I said yes, and shortly thereafter I was in Romanian language training. My wife did not share my Romanian enthusiasms and shortly before we were due to depart in the summer of 1983, she filed for divorce.

This put the United States Government in something of a quandary; for obvious reasons it was the policy not to send single officers to communist countries. Perhaps because of the length of time the position had been vacant or the amount of money invested in my training or the fact that I was now a single parent with a three-year-old daughter in tow or the difficulty in finding on short notice an officer willing and able to go to Romania or perhaps some combination of all four reasons, an exception to the policy was made in my case. So it was late in the summer of 1983 that my daughter, Charlotte, and I headed for Bucharest.

Few readers of these words will need to be informed about the conditions in Romania in the 1980s. No country in the world can be totally independent with an autarchic economy. In the 1980s, it was Romania's tragic fate to be one of these otherwise blessed lands. Threatened by pressing international debts and encouraged to strive for autarky, the country under the leadership of the Ceauşescus embarked on a mad scheme to import a minimum of goods and export anything that could be sold. By the time we arrived, this misconceived policy had completely dislocated the country's economy and forced the consuming public to its knees. No one who lived in this economic nightmare will ever forget the rationing, the long lines of patient, hungry citizens waiting for basic foodstuffs that were often sold out before their turn came around. The energy crisis resulted in long lines of cars at filling stations. Apartments and public buildings went largely unheated. I recall attending a concert at the Atheneul Român one winter evening where the musicians in the string section were all wearing gloves with the fingers cut out. The dark, dimly lit streets made night driving a hazardous enterprise. As gas was even more irregular than electricity, the embassy outfitted our houses with all manner of space heaters and microwave ovens. I remember preparing for a sit-down dinner party when the gas turned off half an hour before the first guest arrived and my struggling to concoct some dinner for twelve that could be cooked in a microwave oven.

Of course, our privileged diplomatic position allowed us to draw down on military stores from the American forces in Germany, and regularly every two months a U. S. Air Force C-54 landed at Otopeni with American foodstuffs: meat and fresh fruits and vegetables. Nevertheless, Romania was "a greater hardship post" with additional allowances and vacation time out of the country. It was a short assignment, just two years, but even so Washington had trouble staffing the post. Not a few assigned there found reasons to request a curtailment. One American secretary arrived on a Friday evening after business hours, took a look around that weekend and reported for duty the following Monday morning with a message in hand for Washington requesting curtailment.

The thought of curtailment never entered my mind for several reasons. Perhaps first it was because Romania seemed to be the purpose of my professional life which directly and indirectly had been focused on the rivalry between the West and the communist world. My years as a naval officer two decades before, the eighteen years in the reserves, the subsequent years in diplomacy as an American Foreign Service Officer had all been affected by Soviet communism. Now at last I was in the belly of the beast. I was convinced or perhaps I had convinced myself that what I did was important; and if I did it well, I could make a real difference in events and some people's lives, a rare reward in a bureaucracy as vast as the United States Government. Whether there was scrap of truth in all this, or it was totally delusional, others not I will determine. There was as well the exhilaration of trying to outwit the Securitate, which seemed determined to minimize any American influence or impact on Romania or indeed any American contact at all with the Romanian people. Thus it was that no thought of curtailment ever occurred to me, and at the end of the stipulated two years I extended for an additional year, and at the end of the third year I extended for a virtually unheard of fourth. Sometime later I tried to use the four years as leverage only to be curtly informed, "I don't think you understand, Dr. Latham, how this is viewed in Washington: three years a hero, four years a lunatic."

A few words about the American Embassy in Bucharest in the mid 1980s may be useful to set my file into its contemporary context. The United States, a leading member of the North Atlantic Treaty

Organization (NATO) and the Romanian Socialist Republic, a member, however reluctant and uncooperative, in the Warsaw Treaty Organization (WTO) were in opposing military alliances. The American president during my time in the embassy was Ronald Reagan, a conservative, somewhat populist Republican with little sympathy for communists or communism. The president of Romania was Nicolae Ceauşescu, also General Secretary of the Romanian Communist Party. His precise ideology was difficult to discern; it was generally described as a mixture of Romanian nationalism and Stalinist communism. Some pundits styled it national communism. His administration depended heavily on members of his own extended family and individuals from the region of his birth, Oltenia. Prominently among his associates in the administration was his wife, Elena, who sat on the Central Committee, among other honors. Their precise relationship remains shadowy. It appears that they had divided up responsibilities by topic: his primary responsibilities appeared to be national defense, foreign affairs, and most aspects of the economy; hers were apparently personnel in general, especially party cadre, professional assignments, education and culture broadly defined. These last two portfolios touched directly on my work as a cultural attaché.

The bilateral relationship was more complicated than a simple dichotomy would imply. To the degree that Romanian nationalism urged independence from the lockstep, pro-Soviet military posture of the Warsaw Pact and from the preconceived economic development planning of COMECON, the United States heartily cheered the Romanians on. Furthermore, we were prepared to reward this behavior with high level visits, flattering press releases and the more substantive trade benefits of MFN (Most Favored Nation), an agreement signed in 1975, which allowed Romanian goods to enter the United States at the same rates as were granted to our most favored trading partners. The attractions of the MFN considerably withered over time as the American Congress began to condition renewal of the MFN status on Romanian respect for human rights. The Congressional hearings focused on Romanian emigration, largely ethnic Germans wishing to go to the Federal Republic and Jews seeking to leave for Israel, Western Europe and North America. No less at issue was religious freedom, the importation of Bibles and Protestant religious life free from harassment by Romanian authorities. In time, the Congressional hearings accompanying MFN renewal became such an onerous embarrassment to the regime that Ceauşescu voluntarily renounced the MFN relationship in 1988.

I served under two ambassadors during the four years I was assigned to Bucharest. The first was David Funderburk (b. 1944), an academic and a political appointee with close ties to conservative Republican circles in North Carolina, especially Senator Jesse Helms. When President Reagan appointed Funderburk ambassador to Bucharest at age 37, he was one of the youngest ambassadors in modern American diplomatic history. He was also one of the most qualified. He had studied European history since his undergraduate years. As he progressed through graduate studies, his interests increasingly settled on Romanian diplomatic history. He studied the Romanian language while still in the United States and in 1971-1972 did research in Romania as a Fulbright scholar. He received his Ph.D. in 1974 from the University of South Carolina. His dissertation title was *British Policy towards Romania, 1938-40*. Both he and his wife, Betty, who had accompanied him in 1971 to Romania, spoke fluent Romanian. His term as ambassador began October 13, 1981, and terminated on May 13, 1985.

The second ambassador, Roger Kirk (b. 1930), came with an entirely different background. He was a career Foreign Service Officer. He had served under both Republican and Democratic administrations; if he had any partisan political feelings, I never saw or heard of them. He inherited a tradition of national service. His father was Admiral Alan

Goodrich Kirk (1888-1963), a career naval officer, (U.S.N.A – Annapolis 1909). He was the American naval attaché in London in 1939 to 1941 when he was appointed Director of the Office of Naval Intelligence. In the Second World War he was the senior American naval officer in theater planning the amphibious landings in Sicily, Italy and at Normandy on D-Day. After the war he retired and began a diplomatic career as ambassador to Belgium (1946-9), the Soviet Union (1949-51) and Taiwan (1962-63). After completing his military obligation as an Air Force officer, Roger Kirk entered the Foreign Service as a career diplomat. He was ambassador to Somalia (1973-5) and Deputy U.S. Representative at IAEA (1978-83). He presented his credentials in Romania on November 29, 1985; he terminated in that position on July 5, 1989.

A few words about my own position in the embassy may be useful. Contrary to my file and the firm belief of the Securitate officers who contributed to it, I was not and have never been an employee of the Central Intelligence Agency (CIA) or any other intelligence organizations; throughout my four years in our Bucharest embassy I was the cultural attaché and as such an employee of the United States Information Agency (USIA). The only exceptions to that were during the Funderburk years when he intermittently appointed me Acting Deputy Chief of Mission. As cultural attaché, I relied on the Department of State and the ambassador for policy guidance and the general context within which I worked, but for resources and a career trajectory I was beholden to the United States Information Agency (USIA). It was known overseas as the United States Information Service (USIS), as the translation of "agency" has pejorative connotations in many languages. USIA was founded in 1953 by President Eisenhower "to understand, inform, and influence foreign publics in promotion of the national interest and to broaden the dialogue between Americans and U.S. institutions and their counterparts abroad." It reflected a growing realization that beyond the diplomatic,

political and military rivalry with the Soviet Union there was an intellectual and ideological challenge as well, a challenge the State Department
and conventional diplomacy were ill prepared to meet. Some way had to
be found for the United States Government to bypass foreign govern-
ments and communicate directly with foreign publics, especially elites
and intellectual leaders. The way that was found was the semi-independ-
ent USIA with its own specialized corps of Foreign Service Officers, its
own budget that at the height of the Cold War exceeded two billion dollars annually and its rather jejune and naïve motto "Telling America's
story to the world." With the Cold War over, USIA was abolished in
1999. It functions were returned to the Department of State, except the
Voice of America, which was placed under an independent Board of
Government Broadcasting.

At the embassy level, the work of public diplomacy – or put more
crassly public relations and propaganda – is under the supervision of the
public affairs officer (PAO), whose immediate assistants are the cultural
attaché (cultural affairs officer – CAO) and the press attaché (information officer – IO). The press attaché is responsible for all fast media,
i.e. all broadcasting, daily newspapers and news journals, usually week-
lies. He is responsible for informing the embassy and Washington about
the contents of such media and trends in public opinion. The cultural
attaché's mandate is more complicated. He is concerned with slow media, i.e. monthlies, specialized publications and books. He overseas cultural and academic exchanges, America Houses, American libraries and
reading rooms and all official relations with artists, authors, academics
and all manner of intellectuals.

Serving in the communist world in general and in Romania specifically brought particular challenges to the work of a cultural attaché. In
all communist countries there was a constant surveillance and, at least
officially, a sense of hostility and restriction. Thus, it was a cat-and-

mouse game with the authorities. You were constantly looking for opportunities to communicate with the local population; the authorities were constantly pushing back and finding ways to curtail such communication. As cultural relations in all communist countries were governed by a specific written agreement periodically renewed, the local authorities inevitably insisted that all exchanges be regulated and administered on a government-to-government basis. The largest of the exchanges was the Fulbright Program, elsewhere administered by a bi-national commission, usually composed of academics. As there were no such bi-national commissions permitted in the communist countries, the task of selecting all the Fulbrighters going to the United States fell to the cultural attaché who usually had to select and interview candidates from lists handed him by the local ministry of education. Conversely, the cultural attaché had to help in the selection of the American candidates who would be teaching English, doing research or conducting university courses in the host country. Once the candidates had arrived, the cultural attaché was responsible for seeing to their welfare in general and resolving the manifold problems for them and their families that arose throughout the academic year. To help me with these responsibilities, I had two assistant American cultural attaches: one assistant, Jim Morgan, had the sole duty to administer the academic exchanges and the other assistant, Kiki Munshi, largely functioned as the head librarian at the large and busy American library.

What made cultural work in Romania in the 1980s particularly challenging and, therefore, interesting proceeded from three unique but interrelated facts. The first was the rapidly declining standard of living that resulted from Ceauşescu's obsessive drive to pay off the national debt by boosting exports and seeking an autarchic economy. These efforts resulted in food rationing, in long lines at markets, in darkened streets and frigid homes. These measures destroyed whatever lingering loyalty people may have had to the government and to socialist idealism. As one wag observed to me, "This situation here is so desperate, even the village idiot knows the system isn't working!"

Thus a hypocrisy was endemic throughout Romania, and Romanians knew all too well the follies of their country but continued to pledge their allegiance to a government they didn't trust and a social system utterly bankrupt. This came vividly to my attention in a conversation with a ranking party member. I was trying to make a point. Considering what I believed to be my interlocutor's ideology, I framed my remarks in line with Marxist theory, perhaps alluding to class conflict or the labor theory of value. My partner immediately cut me off, "Don't do that! Don't ever do that in Romania! Never forget that there are more Marxists in the Sorbonne than there will ever be in Romania!"

With this hypocrisy came its fraternal twin corruption. Again, a conversation early in my tour brought corruption sharply into focus. Being a cultural attaché in a communist country and modeling myself on the efforts of my colleagues in the Moscow embassy, I tried to sniff out the underground literature. A Romanian poet I knew seemed to be a good place to start, so I tried to steer our conversation in that direction. He knew immediately what I wanted and replied, "Oh, you're asking about samizdat, the stuff that Russian poets read to each other on weekends at their dachas in the country. It's totally unimportant as a form of dissent, and we don't waste our time with it in Romania." He broke into a wide grim and added, "Corruption is our dissent!" I quickly learned just how right he was. I thought I knew something about corruption, indeed I fancied myself something of an expert on the subject. After all I had been born in the Archdiocese of Boston in the heyday of the "Purple Shamrock", James Michael Curley; I had worked in law enforcement for three years in Mayor Daley's Chicago; my first assignment in the Foreign Service was in Beirut at the time of the Intra Bank scandal. I considered

myself something of a connoisseur of corruption, but nothing had prepared me for Romania.

The heart of the problem seemed to spring from the value of the
local currency, the Leu – plural Lei, which was practically worthless.
The communist government set an arbitrary exchange rate of around ten
or twelve lei to the American dollar while a couple of hundred miles to
the west, the Creditanstalt Bank in Vienna was selling around a hundred
lei for a dollar. In this situation of fictional values, society still needed a
reliable standard of value, and it settled on Kent 100s cigarettes. Why it
was Kent 100s and not regular Kents or Marlboros or some other cigarette or something entirely different, I was never able to learn.

We had a Fulbright economics professor from New York in 1983
who was in Romania researching market basket exchange rates. At a
Thanksgiving Day dinner, I asked him how his work was coming along.
He told me he hadn't thought about market basket exchanges rates for
the last two months. He had instead focused entirely on the role of Kent
100s cigarettes. Excitedly, he explained that the world hadn't experienced this kind of value assignment since gold became the universally
accepted standard of value, probably sometime in the eighth millennium
B. C. This Kent 100s phenomenon attracted the attention of the *Wall
Street Journal,* and they sent out a team of two journalists to Bucharest
to research the story which later was reported on the front page of the
newspaper.

The use of Kent 100s appeared in all kinds of transactions. For example, I could fill my car and its reserve tank for two or three packs. And
this was true not only for small personal exchanges. The Romanian Foreign Ministry had a club for foreign diplomats on a lake north of Bucharest. One year our Marine contingent rented the club for the annual ball
celebrating the founding of the Marine Corps. They paid the rent to the
ministry in cartons of Kent 100s.

After hypocrisy and corruption, the third fact to challenge and interest a cultural attaché was the increasing absurdities and monomaniacal posturing of the Ceauşescu family. For the Romanians, it was bad enough to be within the Eastern Block and thus separated from their Latin cousins in Western Europe, from their Francophile traditions, and for many from the universities and cultural institutions of their tertiary education. What made it worse was the silly bombast of the Ceauşescu family, the president's portraits holding a mace or his self-styled title as the "Lion of the Carpathians." Even more ridiculous was his wife, Elena, who does not appear to have ever graduated from primary school, parading herself as a world class scientist in macromolecular chemistry. She compounded this fiction by getting herself elected to various scientific societies. Her vast public roles included membership on the Central Committee in complete violation of the communist tradition that spouses be practically invisible or at least inconspicuous. Not content with such gestures in Bucharest, the family took its clown act on the road and paraded its claims and pretentions in world capitals to include London and Washington.

By the time I took up residence in Bucharest, not only was Romania pitied for its self-induced poverty but as well for its arbitrary, tyrannical and absurd government. It was the butt of jokes, scorn and ridicule not only in the West but no less among its ostensible friends and allies in the East. By 1983 the Romanians seemed to be ashamed, humiliated and completely unsure of themselves. In that Romanian depression there were opportunities to raise Romanian morale and hopefully in the process increase their affection and respect for the United States.

Some of my efforts were trivial. One evening in 1985 I stopped by the diplomatic store on the way home to get a bottle of wine for dinner. It was a 1974 Cabernet Sauvignon from Babadag, and it was excellent. The next morning I was on the steps of the diplomatic store before it opened; and when it did, I bought every case they had, some eight or nine I recall. For the next several months I broke with the custom of serving American or West European wines at dinners and poured my Romanian guests the Babadag cabernet with the label carefully wrapped with a cloth. I then would ask my guests to guess what the wine was. They never did, but when they learned the origin of the wine, I think they were a bit pleased that something Romanian was accepted and appreciated by a foreigner.

Considerably more significant were our efforts at assembling an exhibit on the Miorița, the iconic Romanian ballad. One summer day in 1985 as I sat in my office on Strada Snagov in Bucharest thinking of ways to get over, under or around the communist regime and its tyrannical Council of Culture, my eyes fell on a box of slides of Romania which the Assistant Cultural Attaché and director of the American Library had sent over for me to look at. They were the work of the American photographer Laurence Salzmann. In 1981 Salzmann had been in Romania on an IREX (International Research and Exchange Commission) scholarship and had lived for part of the time in Poiana Sibiului, a small, isolated village of transhumance shepherds 40 kilometers due west of Sibiu. The Salzmann photographs, as I quickly saw, illustrated with particular beauty and poignancy the timeless, unchanging life of these shepherds. It was precisely these qualities that I recalled in the Miorița I had first met when I was studying Romanian in Washington. Somehow it all came together in my mind, and the idea of an American exhibit of the Miorița was born. Eventually a selection of some 38 photographs was made and captioned in sequence with the text of the Miorița in Romanian accompanied by a new translation into English by my assistant Kiki Munshi and myself.

The idea of such an exhibit in Romania in the midst of the Cold War had an immense appeal to me as a solution to my problems with

American exhibits getting acceptance from the Romanian Council of Culture. We would thereby hoist the Council on its own petard. It could accept the exhibit for display throughout the country and risk the considerable enthusiasm we believed it would generate among the Romanian audiences that we hoped would flock to see it. This enthusiasm would then in time produce a respect for American culture and Americans who had searched out and visibly appreciated an element in Romanian culture which was not, after all, well-known or appreciated beyond the borders of Romania.

On the other hand, the Council of Culture could see through this scheme and reject the exhibit for a Romanian tour. We were prepared to profit from that too. If the Council refused permission for a Miorița exhibit, it would be rejecting a major icon of Romanian culture. It would stand naked and exposed as the anti-cultural, indeed anti-Romanian, institution we believed it to be.

To keep the stakes high we did everything possible in such a controlled society to publicize the up-coming exhibit. We talked it up wherever and whenever we could. We distributed the exhibit poster which featured a composite of Salzmann photographs on one side and on the other the Romanian text with the new English translation we had worked on. We went up to Poiana Sibiului one weekend to distribute the poster to the people that Salzmann had photographed only a few years before. The mayor was predictably enthusiastic and promised to use the local schoolhouse to display the exhibit during the annual fair when the transhumance shepherds returned to their homes in Poiana Sibiului. All he required was the permission of the Council of Culture in Bucharest. Lastly, we made a large banner visible all up and down the street outside the American Library announcing the exhibit inside.

The invitations to the *vernissage* went out, and the opening night came round on Monday, 7 April 1986. It was success by any standard.

Many, perhaps most, of those invited came. We opened by the entrance a guest book for people to sign. The entry I remember best, judiciously unsigned, was "We could wait a hundred years for the Soviet embassy to make such an exhibit." That remark convinced me we were on target.

Thus, it was with high expectations that we awaited the general public the next day. And we waited, and we waited, and we waited! The visitors never came. Some of the Romanians who attended the opening night and were known to us personally were called in by some variant of the dreaded Securitate and questioned as to why the Americans had mounted an exhibit on the Miorița. What did it mean and what did they expect to accomplish? One of the pictures featured a laughing shepherd with a steel tooth. Were the Americans perhaps making fun of Romanian dentistry?

The banner flew over the American Library for the following weeks. It did not fly over the lines of impatient visitors we had hoped for, but it silently reminded the many Romans who saw or heard about it that they were being denied access to an exhibit about their national ballad. The point was clearly made and reinforced by repeated broadcasts on the Voice of America and Radio Liberty, the Romanian component of Radio Free Europe: a regime and its Council of Culture which deny their people access to their own national cultural patrimony has severed all ties with the nation and has lost any claim it might have to cultural authority.

On a subsequent visit to the Council of Culture shortly before departing I was invited to take the exhibit with me as it would never be displayed in Romania. Never, in this case, turned out to be about two and a half years when the Revolution of December 1989 left such communist officials and their petty tyrannies only a memory and a warning. The exhibit came out of its crates, toured the country, and returned to its birthplace, Poiana Sibiului.

Not all of our exhibits were thwarted. One in particular I recall was such a success that long lines of visitors snaked out of the building onto a main thoroughfare and around the block. One afternoon, word was passed to the police on the street that a Ceauşescu motorcade was shortly going to pass by. It was clearly going to distress Ceauşescu with unpredictable results to see Romanians lined up patiently to view an American exhibit. The police sensing future trouble ordered the Romanians to turn, face the street and cheer when the motorcade passed. Thus, the exhibit's visitors were instantly converted into an adoring public, and the exhibit continued on without problems.

One effort that did not succeed but proved very gratifying for me at the time and invaluable thereafter grew out of my thwarted efforts to access university students and academics in general. Thinking I might be able to circumvent the bureaucrats of the Ministry of Education by becoming a student myself, I requested permission to enroll in a doctoral program. My embassy agreed on the condition that I must be willing to drop it and walk away if at any point I felt under any pressure on me coming from the Romanian Government. To my surprised delight the Ministry of Education agreed with the stipulation that I would take my degree in the philology department. I protested that I had a strong background in history as an undergraduate and graduate student and had never taken a course in philology in my life. I never did understand the ministry's insistence. Perhaps they feared I might intellectually contaminate a discipline that the communists regarded as being of vital importance on the old Marxist principle, "Who controls the past, controls the future."

Of course, the Securitate or whatever powers there were saw through the scheme immediately, and things were arranged so I had absolutely no contact with Romanian students. Indeed, I set foot only four times in any university building. To further isolate me they brought a professor out of retirement to supervise my dissertation. That proved to be a great gift to me as the professor was the charming and erudite Shakespearian scholar Leon Levițchi. Since we could not meet on university grounds, I determined that we would regularly take lunch at Capșa, then probably the best restaurant in downtown Bucharest. Some of my pleasantest and most enduring memories of Bucharest are the long afternoons spent with Prof. Levițchi over coffee and brandy discussing literature but the conversations ranged over a wide spectrum of subjects. I hope those lunches were some reward for my disturbing his retirement. I hope too that the Securitate officers who planted themselves at nearby tables enjoyed them as well, for my file is replete with receipts for their meals.

I did dip into the file from time to time for my own amusement rather than any academic objective. I was interested to note the surveillance was particularly intense when I was traveling in the country, for example to open an exhibit or visit an American Fulbrighter at a provincial university. In Bucharest, the intensity increased just before I went out of the country or just after I returned. My file makes clear what I already knew or suspected: my telephone was tapped, I was frequently followed, they eaves-dropped on many of my conversations and enlisted an army of informers, all of the Romanian employees at the embassy but as well many of the other Romanians I happened to meet officially or unofficially. Many of my embassy colleagues found the constant surveillance irksome. I did not, perhaps because I had been trained to expect it, and I simply regarded it as the price one had to pay for doing business in Easter Europe,

There was, however, one exception to my indifference. Shortly after we arrived in Bucharest in 1983, I began to notice a disturbing trend. Every evening at 8:30 p.m. the phone rang with a wrong number. For me it was simply an inconvenience; for my daughter who had just fallen asleep, however, it was a major disruption. As every parent of a three-year-old knows, once they are awakened shortly after they have fallen asleep, you have a major problem on your hands. First, they are thirsty and require a glass of water, then they require another bedtime story, then they have to go pee-pee, and finally they must say their bedtime prayers again. All too often it was after 10:00 p.m. before she fell asleep again. Nor was it only a disruption in the evening; the following morning when I tried to get her up and dressed for school, she was still sleepy and cross as a bear. Of course, I knew what was going on. They were checking to see if I was safely home for the night and whoever was responsible for my movements could sign off for day and safely go home himself/herself. Any way this went on for a time, but I finally lost my temper. When I picked up the phone that evening, I loudly reminded whoever was on the other end of the line of my domestic situation and, reverting to the vocabulary of my sailor days, I wished him/her a most unpleasant after-life and I was just advancing on their present life when I heard a click and they hung up. The next night the wrong number call came at 7:00 p.m. as it did the next few nights before they tapered off.

Sometimes the Securitate's attention was rather clumsy and even amusing. For example, we went up to the mountains one weekend. When we returned to our house on Strada Plantelor that Sunday evening, there were cigarette butts on the floor of my daughter's bedroom, very unlikely detritus of a little girls not yet seven and a totally unnecessary reminder that the Securitate was ubiquitous in Romania.

No less amusing was an incident in my office; I was discussing business with the ACAO Kiki Munshi when the Marine guard called to say there was a woman downstairs wishing to speak with the cultural attaché. I went down and escorted her upstairs. It turned out that the rather attractive young lady wanted to write the Romanian-American philosopher Mircea Eliade. I happened to have a copy of *Who's Who in America* and went over to the bookcase to get the professor's address. When I returned to my desk, she extracted from her bag a large brown envelope and proceeded to change the subject. She now wanted to have my opinion as to her chances for a modeling career in the United States. To give force to her question she took from the brown envelope a sheath of pictures of herself stark naked cavorting on some sandy beach much to the embarrassment of ACAO Munshi who was quickly turning beet red. After giving the pictures the studied examination they deserved, I determined that the young lady was qualified for at least two more professions than simply modeling but that the cultural section was not the appropriate place to explore such career options in the United States. So I escorted her back down stairs and left her at the door of the Consulate as the proper place to investigate American visas and professional employment in the United States.

That attempt by the Securitate failing to bring forth the desired result, they pointed their efforts in the opposite direction. One Saturday morning as Charlotte and I were packing to leave for the embassy's weekend club, the villa in Timişu de Jos, the doorbell rang. When I opened the door in pranced the two young men I had talked with at some American Library event the week before. I had assumed they were friends, had given them my card and invited them to drop by sometime for a conversation and a cup of coffee, an invitation I extended as a social gesture to many Romanians knowing it would never be acted on. It was soon apparent that theirs was not a simple friendship and they had some hopes I might join them in their unsimple friendship. I made them the promised coffee and started some idle chitchat wondering how I could bring this embarrassing visit to an end. It occurred to me that I might quickly establish the boundaries of my own personality and see how Charlotte's packing was coming, so I offered to introduce them to my daughter. They clearly had been badly briefed for their enterprise, for the word "daughter" seemed to come as a complete surprise to them. The "pretty boys" quickly pranced back to the door leaving my house and their undrunk cups of coffee. Thus my daughter was denied the pleasure of making their acquaintance, and I was denied the pleasure of ever seeing them again.

These were entirely and cynical set-pieces of the Securitate from which I was well prepared to protect myself. There were also occasions when it was necessary to protect innocent, sometimes naïve Romanians. One December evening I was browsing in a second-hand bookstore on Ştefan cel Mare towards Dorobanţi. The manager knew my interests in Romanian history from earlier visits and offered to introduce me to another customer who had some history books to sell. We met, chatted a bit, and he invited me to his book lined apartment in one of the blocks up Dorobanţi. He made me a cup of tea, and we settled in for a conversation on books. Then I noticed on his desk the picture of a man in the summer dress whites of a naval officer. He was, my host informed me, his brother who had been an officer in the Romanian merchant marine but had been lost at sea. I then unthinkingly mentioned I too had been a naval officer. Knowing from my accent I was a foreigner and suspecting my mother tongue was a Germanic one, he naturally asked if was the navy of the German Democratic Republic, i.e. communist East Germany. When I said it wasn't, he then asked which navy it was. To this I replied, "Believe me, Sir, you don't want to know." As I was sitting in his home, drinking his tea, this was a rather brusque if not rude repayment for his hospitality, and he was clearly taken aback. It took him only a couple of seconds, however, to realize what had happened. His face broke out in a wide smile, and he simply said, "Thank you!" Thus I left him in the comfortable position of plausible denial had I been followed and not in the decidedly uncomfortable position of having had an unsanctioned visit of an American naval officer and diplomat in his home which could have complicated his life by several orders of magnitude. In the end, I bought some books from him. To my regret and doubtless his relief, we never saw each other again.

My love of bookstores of all types and the innocent hours I slew in them or spent gazing in their windows attracted a good deal of the Securitate's attention and speculation. Why this should have been so, however, I have never been able to understand. I should have thought bookstores like libraries, theaters and universities were the natural habitat of cultural attaches. Beyond my own love of and interest in books, shortly after I began work in Romania, a second powerful motive for book collecting emerged. It was soon apparent that the Romanian government was doing some radical pruning of Romanian history in particular and Romanian culture in general. For example, the eighty odd years of the Hohenzollern-Sigmaringen monarchy were distorted and nearly obliterated. The role of Carol I in ushering in a modern state was ignored as was the heroism of King Mihai I in breaking Romania out of the Axis alliance. I have books in my library that have had pictures of the royal family razored out or their names and those of other non-persons blacked out. Nevertheless as a diplomat I was in a position of preserving and protecting some aspects of that national patrimony and then awaiting a happier day. Under these circumstances, I had no choice but do all that I could to defeat these anti-intellectual efforts by using the opportunities my profession gave me. As books were an area I was at home in, I started collecting books on Romanian subjects that failed to meet the regime's standards of acceptability. It was my intention to take them out of Romania and place them in some American institution that would make them publicly available. I must here make absolutely clear that I had no self-aggrandizing vision of myself as an intellectual Jean d'Arc leading an army of truth and integrity in defense of Romanian culture, but I did think I had to make an effort to enlist in that army.

In brief, the public market for second hand books was controlled by the government. Books that people wished to sell were first placed in a central deposit which examined them for acceptability and then farmed them out to the several second hand bookstores around the city. At the deposit offending pictures could be removed and offending passages blacked out. Those offending books not amenable to such simple and superficial editing were simply withdrawn from circulation and disappeared down some ideological black hole. Obviously my scheme to be successful required me to insinuate myself into the choke point at the deposit. This I did at a deposit near the Hotel Union. Every few days I would drop by and be shown the materials otherwise destined for the black hole. It was an arrangement too good to last, and after a couple of months the deposit got word back to me to stop coming around. I suppose the Securitate had followed me one day to the deposit and decided to upset my bibliophilic applecart.

Shortly thereafter, however, a worthy substitute for the deposit appeared in the person of Radu Sterescu. By the time I became acquainted with him, his exploits had become legendary. In the 1980s he was running a black market second hand antiquarian book business out of a small ground floor apartment on a side street off 1 Mai Boulevard, an apartment he shared with numberless books and a comatose mother lying on a couch whose only evidence of life during the time I knew Radu was her very audible, rasping breathing. Radu's whole purpose in life was to care for his mother and to provide second hand books to collectors and scholars, for which I generally paid him in Kent 100s cigarettes. It was said that his stream of American scholar clients went back to Keith Hitchins, the first in the line. It continued on through Glenn Torrey and Glee Wilson to Paul Michelson. The contact was passed from exchange scholar to exchange scholar; finally it was Irina Livizeanu, who introduced Radu to me. In the earlier period Radu was understood to have had a larger apartment elsewhere in Bucharest before the reduced space I knew.

The legend of Radu had many elements. He was said to be veteran of the Royal Romanian Army in the Second World War and at some point to have been the Royal Librarian. At one time he apparently had been involved in gambling and horse racing. Once, the Securitate was closing in on him in some public garden when he had on his person a large sum of money of unclear origin. He unwisely determined to make a run for it, an ambitious if unsuccessful undertaking for a man his age. Perhaps the price of that misbegotten inspiration was his reduced living space. It was uncertain whether Radu had or had not spent time in jail. I'm betting he didn't.

Radu's *modus operandi* was simple. He knew or could imagine the contents of most private libraries in Bucharest worth knowing. When the owner of such a library died or moved and downsized – and there was much moving in those days as Ceausescu cleared whole areas of the city to build his ironically name Palace of the People – Radu would appear ghoul-like on the scene to salvage what books he could profitably use. His knowledge of Romanian bibliography and publishing was vast, and I relied on him repeatedly for advice and help. I remember one day he thrust into my hands a copy of Lucian Predescu's *Enciclopedia Cugetarea* (Bucureşti: Cugetarea – Georgescu Delafras, 1940) with the curt order, "Buy it! You will need it!" Once I said I would like to have Franz Joseph Sulzer's *Geschichte des Transalpinischen Daciens* (Wien: Rudolph Graeffer, 1781) for the sake of the map of Bucharest, reputedly the first map ever of the city, in the first volume. Never did I expect he would be ever able to produce a work over two hundred years old. In less than a month he had it minus the third volume but including the invaluable map in volume I.

One can only speculate how Radu got away with his totally illegal enterprise. Surely the Securitate knew about it and had followed many a Westerner to Radu's front door. The simple explanation is that the foreigners were buying books that the Securitate didn't want circulating in the country anyway and taking them out of the country, good riddance! Bill Edwards, our press attaché, had a more subtle explanation. He believed the Securitate, always more nationalist than communist, realized that Radu's clients had deep commitments to Romania and Romanian culture; and the Securitate wanted to do and to tolerate what was possible to encourage this good will. There was third possibility that occurred to me one Saturday afternoon after a visit to Radu's. For obvious reasons no foreigner would want to draw attention to himself when calling on Radu, a reluctance even greater in the case of a Romanian. Thus it was on this occasion I was unhappy to see when I arrived that there was another customer there already who was even more discomforted than I was. To make matters worse it was someone that I thought I had seen somewhere before, and he appeared to recognize me. It was only later driving home that I realized that the customer I had seen was Ştefan Andrei, the Romanian Foreign Minister. Clearly Radu had friends in high places. Radu was a rascal and would have been a rascal in any society, in any era, under any government; but he was a loveable and a useful rascal. He will always stand out in my memory as one of the great heroes – perhaps better said anti-heroes – of the Cold War, and many a library in the United States, including mine, is richer for his efforts.

When I finished my tour in Bucharest, I was posted on to Athens. That was altogether agreeable as it was close enough to Romania to allow frequent returns. In 1988 I apparently went on the stop-list and couldn't get a visa. Nothing so brusque as a refusal, the Romanians are too polite for that and too smart to want the complications that would ensue from refusing an American diplomat a visa. Whenever I called the

Romanian consulate in Athens, I was told the request was pending in Bucharest and the visa would doubtless appear in two weeks. It did not appear in two weeks nor in two months, and it was nearly two years when I got a call in November 1989 that my visa had arrived. So I returned at the end of the month and into the first week of the fateful December 1989. I went again as soon as the frontiers opened in January 1990 and later that year to celebrate the first Easter in a free Romania. I have been back many times since.

I returned to Washington in 1990 and retired from the Foreign Service in 1993. My life since then has been largely preoccupied with Romania and the bilateral relationship. I gave among other things a series of lectures on Romania at the Smithsonian Institution. For several years I returned to the State Department on contract and supervised the Advanced Areas Studies Course on Romania and Moldova at the National Foreign Affairs Training Center – Foreign Service Institute (NFATC-FSI). I was inducted into the American Romanian Academy of Arts and Sciences. For a number of years I was the Academy's secretary, and in 2000 I won the Academy's book prize for a work on the Miorița and the exhibit described above. Between 2000 and 2002 I was a Fulbright professor at the universities of Bucharest and Babeș-Bolyai in Cluj-Napoca leading graduate seminars on the Cold War and American history. I have written a number of books, articles and reviews generally focused on the cultural interfaces between Romania and the English-speaking world. Thus, my retirement has been immensely enriched by my Romanian experiences but most especially by a twenty-five year friendship and ultimately a marriage to my wife, the Romanian poet and playwright Ioana Ieronim, whom I first met in 1992 when she was the cultural counselor of the Romanian Embassy in Washington.

Now I can look back on more than forty years of interest in and fascination with Romania, Romanians and Romanian culture broadly defined. Here I'm reminded of Bob Hope's old theme song, "Thanks for the Memories." A man meets up with his old lover and recalls their times together, observing "You may have been a headache, but you never were a bore!" That about sums up my memories which have been brought forcefully forward while working on this introduction and reviewing my file. These forty years have been educational, exciting, enlightening, frequently amusing and never boring. One may safely conclude that they were a personal success. Never before or since have I gone to work in the morning not knowing for sure what would happen that day. It was a wonderful feeling.

That, however, begs the question of whether they were a success seen from the perspective of the Romanians or the American taxpayers who had to foot the rather expensive bill for most of my time in Romania. That, of course is a question for the Romanians and the other Americans to answer, not me. What difference, positive or negative, did my work in Romania make? What opinions if any were changed or at least modified? What events were shaped differently because I was or had been there? There are probably several valid answers to these questions. It may be that this, my file, provides one such answer.

I am sometimes asked if I have ever had any contact after reading my file with any of the people who had been reporting, and the answer is extensive, repeated contact. The so-called friendships then in many cases are sincere friendships now. When the subject of their reporting and my file comes up as it occasionally does, we generally laugh about it. There are no hard feelings. They were doing what their government demanded and their families' welfare required. I knew that they would be reporting their contact with me, and they knew that I knew. It was a strange case of I knew that they knew that I knew that they knew that I knew that they knew and so on into infinity like two facing mirrors. After I had requested my file but before I had gotten it, I was in conversation with a Romanian diplomat I had known during the communist period. He indicated that the file would indeed make for interesting reading but cautioned that some of the reports on me would be sheer fiction and some mendacious half-truths. But some would be accurate, complete and insightful. Then he stopped, smiled and added, "And I know because I wrote them myself."

I must conclude with some words of gratitude. First, of course, to the first editor, Dr. Vadim Guzun, whose efforts turned a chaotic mass of material into a readable Romanian edition of this book (*Dosarul de Securitate al unui Diplomat American, Ernest H. Latham, Jr. 1979-1987*; București: Editura Militară, 2017). His was truly labor in the vineyard at midday. I must also thank the officers and staff of Editura Militară whose faith in the editor and the subject allowed them to commit to publishing the book sight unseen and whose technical skills insured that it finally saw the light of printer's ink. Once again, I am reminded of my everlasting debt to my wife Ioana whose comments and advice in all matter Romanian have helped me in my contributions to this book and whose linguistic skills insured an accurate and beautiful translation of this introduction in the Romanian edition. Now it is my pleasure to add my thanks to Prof. Dennis Deletant, who edited the English edition of the book, to Mihai Moroiu who translated the documents from their Romanian originals, and Histria Books and its staff for publishing the English edition you now hold in your hands. Lastly, I would be remiss indeed if I failed to thank those officers of the Securitate that I never met but occasionally saw for their painstaking, meticulous efforts to provide me with a diary of my time in Romania, the diary that my own government discouraged me from keeping. I hope now with these words of appreciation they will be encouraged to make themselves known to me, for I should very much enjoy a reunion where we can reminisce together. As of this writing on September 25, 2020, they have not contacted me.

American-Romanian Political and Cultural Relations during the Cold War

"Our genuine encounter with the West can be built on cultural pillars."

— Informant "Ionescu", 1986

After the communist takeover of Romania and its absorption into the Soviet bloc, the country was no exception in the nearly total subordination of its national interests to Moscow. Relations with the United States followed the same path, within the wider framework of East-West relations. After World War II, the Petru Groza government was recognized by the United States and peace treaties were signed with Romania, Italy, Bulgaria and Hungary as erstwhile members of the Axis Pact.

Cultural, scientific and educational relations between Romania and the United States could not be separated from political and economic relations; on the contrary, given the potential for propaganda and counterpropaganda in those fields, they were duly required to follow the contemporary ideological requirements. Despite the tense political relationship, the United States opened an office in Bucharest in 1946 to promote

American culture. It included a library, a ball hall, and a theater to show documentary movies.[1]

A note of protest that the American Mission in Bucharest addressed to the (still Royal) Ministry of Foreign Affairs on August 16, 1947, illustrates the complex challenges surrounding the first post-war attempts to develop bilateral relations, including cultural relations. The note stated, "The Mission has been placed under the surveillance of police of the Romanian Government," who "interrogated and arrested several persons who were leaving the Mission."[2]

Fig. 1. Bucharest, A.I. Vyshinsky, General I.Z. Susaikov, P. Groza, Gh. Gheorghiu-Dej, L. Pătrăşcanu, after the festive celebrations organized on the occasion of the reunion of northern Transylvania with "democratic Romania," 1945 (F.O.C.R.)[3].

---

[1]Mircea Răceanu, *Cronologie comentată a relaţiilor româno-americane: de la începutul cunoaşterii reciproce până la prăbuşirea regimului comunist din România, 1989*, Foreword by Ernest H. Latham Jr., afterword by Dennis Deletant, Bucharest, Editura Silex, 2005, p.163. See also Sorin Aparaschivei, *Spionajul american în România, 1944-1948*, Bucharest, Editura Militară, 2013, pp. 230-131.

[2]Archives of the Romanian Ministry of Foreign Affairs (abbreviated A.M.A.E.), and "*Dosare Speciale. S.U.A.*", box 220/1-4/1964-1967, file 3, unpaginated.

[3]The source of these photographs is the *Online Photoarchive of Romanian Communism* (abbreviated F.O.C.R.), visited at http://www.arhivelenationale.ro/ fototeca/, on August 1, 2017.

Things became ever worse when Romania's process of Sovietization and Stalinization was in full swing, when the political opposition was annihilated, and all adversaries were eliminated physically, including the "reactionary" social categories. The low point was reached in March 1950 when a deputy Romanian Foreign Minister verbally communicated to the American Minister in Bucharest the official request that the Office of Information of the United States Legation cease its activities immediately.[4]

The Americans asked to be informed about the reasons for this measure, and the Romanian Ministry of Foreign Affairs answered, in the name of the government of the People's Republic of Romania, by *note verbale* No. 870, on April 14, 1950, which mentioned, among other things, that the U.S.I.S. had engaged in espionage "under its pretended cultural activity," and the books, press, film, and other events it organized, "have spread backward ideas, professed racial discrimination, contained slanders against peace and liberty-loving peoples, such as the Romanian People's Republic and openly fomented war"[5].

The U.S. Government answered with *note verbale* No. 925 of April 26, 1950 of the legation in Bucharest, denying any espionage activity, rejecting all of the Romanian allegations and reproaching Romania for its ongoing unfriendly behavior towards the United States. Nevertheless, the situation remained as imposed by Romania unilaterally, contrary to diplomatic practice and the usually considerate attitude of a host country.[6] In response, the United States closed Romania's commercial office

---

[4] A.M.A.E., *Dosare Speciale. S.U.A.*, box 220/13-24/1946, file 13, unpaginated.

[5] Ibidem.

[6] Ibidem.

in New York on the same day.[7] The puppet regime of Bucharest answered that spring by taking action against the Romanian employees of the American Information Office in typical Stalin-era style: changes were fabricated, they were subjected to inhumane criminal investigations, and arbitrary sentencing.[8]

A report, ordered by Ana Pauker, Romania's Foreign Minister, on the American Library of the U.S.A. Mission is particularly significant for the cessation of cultural relations between the two countries.[9] It started from the assumption that the Library, "aimed at supporting and promoting in our country American publications and books, and to keep our so-called U.S.A. sympathizers informed on American ideas and life style." The document maintained that "the office is more than a library, for it does not offer only books, but it also screens documentary films, opens U.S.A. photo exhibitions, concerts of recorded music, and newspapers and journals are also made available." "It is self-evident that the purpose is to spread American propaganda under the guise of culture" was the conclusion of the unknown author in the Romanian Ministry of Foreign Affairs, on November 26, 1949.[10]

The withdrawal of the Soviet troops stationed in Romania (1958) ushered in a new stage in Romanian-American relations and resumed the previous dialogue. The brutal closing of the American Library was forgotten and, on December 9, 1960, the first bilateral agreement on culture,

---

[7]Mircea Răceanu, Cronologie comentată..., op. cit., p. 173.

[8] See Annie Samuelli, *The Wall Between*, Robert B. Luce (editor), Washington, D.C., 1967; Ernest H. Latham Jr., *Timeless and Transitory. 20th Century Relations between Romania and the English-Speaking World*, Bucharest, Editura Vremea, 2012, pp. 453-455.

[9]The American Library was at 12 Strada Dianei, Bucharest.

[10]A.M.A.E., *Dosare Speciale. S.U.A.*, box 220/13-24/1946, file 13, unpaginated.

education, and science was concluded. The cultural exchanges between the two countries had legal underpinnings, such as the Memorandum between the Academy of the Socialist Republic of Romania and America's National Academy of Sciences,[11] or the agreement between Romania's National Council of Scientific Research and the U.S. International Research & Exchanges Board (IREX).[12] They started the exchanges of students, researchers, and visiting professors; several books on the subject were published in both countries, mutual exhibitions, and visits of experts in various fields started being organized.

The visit of President Richard M. Nixon to Bucharest[13] was the first by an American president to a socialist state, preceded by the fact that Romania did not participate in the Soviet-led military intervention in Czechoslovakia in the summer of 1968[14]: these events contributed to an impressive "brandishing" of Ceauşescu's image, and it brought Romania heightened prestige in the world. The resumption of diplomatic relations on February 6, 1946, did not mean, however, progress in Romanian-American relations beyond the limitations imposed on members of the Soviet bloc after World War II, that is, beyond the interests of the giant to Romania's east. [15]

---

[11]Concluded in 1966.

[12]Concluded in 1968.

[13]August 2-3, 1969. This visit was preceded by Nixon's unofficial visit in 1967. N. Ceauşescu's first state visit to the United States was on October 26-27, 1970.

[14]August 21, 1968. The participants were the Soviet Union, Poland, East Germany, Bulgaria and Hungary.

[15]The Treaty of Friendship, Cooperation and Mutual Assistance between the Romanian People's Republic and the Union of Socialist Soviet Republics was signed in Moscow on February 4, 1948.

Fig. 2. Bucharest, Gh. Gheorghiu-Dej, P. Groza (speaking) with Gh.
Tătărescu, General C. Vasiliu-Rășcanu, upon return their from Moscow,
where they were granted "support" in grains, 1945 (F.O.C.R.).

President Nixon's visit had mainly a political significance, as it sym-
bolized an unprecedented zenith in the bilateral relationship, but it also
had a cultural component, the opening of an American library in Bucharest and a Romanian library in New York.[16] Moreover, an Agreement on
cooperation and exchanges in the cultural, educational, scientific and
technological fields between Romania and the United States was signed
in Bucharest on December 13, 1974.[17] The highest level of cooperation

---

[16]Constantin Moraru, "Evoluția relațiilor româno-americane. Importanța întâlnirilor la nivel
înalt", by Nicolae Ecobescu (editor), *România: supraviețuire și afirmare prin diplomație în anii
Războiului Rece*, vol. II, Bucharest, Fundația Europeană Titulescu, 2013, pp. 624-626, 629. The
granting of the Most Favored Nation clause to Romania was followed by President Gerald Ford's
visit to Bucharest, on August 2-3, 1975.

[17]Renewed for another 5 years in December 1979. See A.M.A.E., collection U.S.A./1985, file
1336, p. 83.

was reached on July 28, 1975, when Congress passed the Most Favored Nation clause for commercial relations with Romania[18].

Ronald Reagan's presidency, from its start in 1981, and the international political climate,[19] marked the beginning of a deterioration in the bilateral relationship, worsened by Romania's internal problems: the growth of the country's foreign debt, an accelerated degradation of its standard of living, breaches of human rights, restrictions of religious rights, curtailed foreign travel and emigration. The following years led to marked regression in Romanian-American relations, to the point of direct confrontation and Romanian opposition to the considerable improvement in the American-Soviet relations at the time of the *Perestroika*.

A cable from the Ministry of Foreign Affairs to the Romanian Embassy in Washington DC listed the main issues for attention in 1983 (the year when the American cultural attaché, Ernest Hargreaves Latham, Jr. was assigned to his post in Bucharest): keeping the Most Favored Nation clause; economic developments in the United States and opportunities to increase exports to America; the presidential and congressional election campaigns; Romanian-American relations in general.[20]

Neither in 1983 nor in any of the following years were cultural relations mentioned. Thus, there are not many diplomatic sources on the subject available The few documents available reveal the fact that Bucharest considered only one cultural aspect to be of interest: propaganda. Visits, books, translations, publications, exhibits, performances, movies,

---

[18]See details in Mircea Răceanu, *Istoria clauzei naţiunii celei mai favorizate în relaţiile româno-americane*, Bucharest, Institutul Naţional pentru Memoria Exilului Românesc, 2009.

[19]Primarily, the Soviet military interference in Afghanistan.

[20]A.M.A.E., *S.U.A.*/1983, file 1781, p.20, cable M.A.E. nr. 5/02565 din 15 iunie 1983.

documentaries, academic exchanges, all cultural or scientific activities, the expansion of Romanian-American exchanges were only valued for their use as propaganda to create an idealized image of the regime.[21] The most significant initiatives could only be taken with "higher approval."[22]

Given this kind of "progress" in the development of bilateral cultural-scientific exchanges, in October of 1985, the U.S.I.A. director pointed out to the Romanian ambassador in Washington the fact that Romania "does not take full advantage of the provisions in the exchange program, particularly those concerning Chapter I-Education," and gave as examples: "lecturer positions remain unoccupied, no Romanian experts have been appointed for various research programs, Romanian professors have not been sent to American universities to establish chairs of Romanian language and literature or of Romanian history and civilization."[23]

---

[21]See, for instance, A.M.A.E., *S.U.A./*1985, file 1340, p.79, Romania's Ministry of Foreign Affairs (abbreviated M.A.E.) cable No. 5/01838, April 29, 1985, to the embassy in Washington.

[22]Ibidem, file 1340, p. 110, note of the Department for Foreign Cultural Relations No. 5711 of May 30, 1985. The marginal importance given to cultural relations can be seen also in the M.A.E. note of November 10, 1986 (no number) on talking points for the Romanian officials to use with Deputy Secretary of State John Whitehead during his visit to Romania, A.M.A.E. *S.U.A./*1986, file 1085, pp. 27-35.

[23]Ibidem, file 1338, pp. 2-3, cable from the embassy in Washington No. 074067 of October 24, 1985.

Fig. 3. Bucharest, the USSR Communist Party delegation led by N. Khrushchev that participated in the 8th Congress of the Romanian Communist Party, 1960 (F.O.C.R.).

U.S.I.A. deputy directors Marvin Remick and Alan Perriman raised the issue again with Romanian diplomatic counselor Mircea Răceanu in Washington, on October 26, 1985: Romania did not exploit the opportunity to send experts in various fields to the United States. Bucharest was further reminded that the country remained behind other socialist states as far as cultural-scientific exchanges were concerned: "East Germany, Poland and Hungary use all the scholarships offered by I.R.E.X.," and there was a "growing number of scientists and cultural representatives from Hungary, East Germany, and Bulgaria who participated in various cultural and scientific programs with the United States."[24]

The communist authorities vehemently rejected any criticism, even if indirect, an example of which is the urgent cable sent by the Romanian Foreign Ministry to the embassy in Washington on January 23, 1986,

[24]Ibidem, file 1336, pp. 67-69, cable of the embassy in Washington No. 074078 of October 26, 1985.

reacting to the fact that the American Library, directed by Melanie S. Munshi,[25] under the responsibility of Ernest H. Latham Jr., had exhibited a news article[26] describing the situation of the mathematician Radu Mihail Roşu[27]. One day after the article was exhibited, the United States charge d'affaires in Bucharest was called in and told, among other things, that publicizing the Roşu problem was "an insult and a provocative action against our country, trespassing against the rules that govern the relations between the foreign embassies in Bucharest and the host country," and demanded to "immediately remove the article from the Library window"[28].

And more than that. In the fall of 1987, the exhibition "Filmul american ieri şi azi" ("American Film Yesterday and Today," which had taken considerable time, effort, and expense to organize, and had been highly

---

[25]M.S. Munshi joined the U.S. Foreign Service in 1980, and held in the course of her career various positions in the U.S. embassies in Nigeria, Romania (1983-1987, 2000-2002), Greece, Sierra Leone, Tanzania and India. See her novel, *Whispers in Bucharest* (Bucharest: Editura Compania, 2014), includes a description of the American Library – one of the main "objectives" of this present edition. She had arrived in September 1983 and found that the American Library was a "bizarre labyrinth of small stair cases, little doors and all kinds of surprises." It appeared to her to have been put together out of "originally two houses belonging to the same family" because they faced each other. The embassy had apparently built the link between them, which housed a theater and cloakroom. There were not only 16 mm, but even 35 mm projectors. The library building faced the offices and the exhibition area. The other spaces included the Blue Room and a kitchen.

[26]The article "Repression in Romania", by Anthony Lewis, *The* International *Herald Tribune* , January 11, 1986.

[27]Authorities denied him his passport.

[28]A.M.A.E., *S.U.A.*/1986, file 1078, p. 14, M.A.E. cable to the embassy in Washington nr. 5/0297 of January 23, 1986.

successful in Bucharest and Timişoara, was closed without any explanation or warning. That initiative followed the fact that, on June 19, 1987, the Romanian Embassy representatives in Washington were approached again by Dell Pendergrast, U.S.I.A. deputy director for the USSR and Eastern Europe, who expressed the Americans' disappointment that the Romanians had such limited participation in the bilateral program of cultural exchanges, having thus reached such a low point; that there remained many unused appointments. He observed that there were no political issues to hinder the cultural-scientific exchanges between the two countries.[29]

Frank Strovas, the American counselor for press and culture, was invited by the Romanian Council of Socialist Culture and Education on October 31, 1987, and he was informed that, "given the local cultural programs already scheduled", the American film exhibition "had been closed, and it could not be reopened in Craiova."[30] This Romanian development was included in the bilateral discussions, already burdened with the above mentioned problems. The American authorities told the Romanian ambassador in Washington that these minor disagreements might have a negative impact on the bilateral relations[31] and expressed the disappointment of the State Department[32].

The cultural relations between the United States and Romania kept declining in the later Ceauşescu years, despite attempts to maintain them,

---

[29]A.M.A.E., *S.U.A.*/1987, file 1043, p. 44, cable of the embassy in Washington No. 073363, of June 19, 1987.

[30]Ibidem, file 1051, vol. II, p. 91, note of the C.C.E.S. (Council of Socialist Culture and Education) to M.A.E., October 31, 1987.

[31]Ibidem, p. 96, cable of the embassy in Washington No. 073651 of November 4, 1987, p. 108.

[32]Idem, p. 108, cable of the embassy in Washington No. 073674 of November 16, 1987.

and that can be also seen from the annual reports of the area office of the Romanian Foreign Ministry. The unpublished 1984-1987 reports of *Direcţia Relaţii V* (Office of Relations V), Chapter "Cultural, Technological and Scientific Relations and Propaganda Activity" is a complementary source along with the pertinent Securitate documents in providing the Romanian point of view.

1984 – "Romania's cultural, technological and scientific relations and propaganda activities in the two Americas better served the aims of Romanian policy and our country's interests in the year 1984. On the one hand, the press and mass media, particularly in the Latin American countries, have presented Romania's domestic and foreign policies favorably and widely and on the other hand activities with a lasting effect were initiated in the USA, Canada, and the Latin American countries, contributing both to the overall development of Romania's relations with those states, but also to make Romania better known in the respective countries.

In this sense, especially to be considered are the activities organized in most of the countries covered by the Office of Relations V on the occasion of the 40th anniversary of the "revolution of social and national, anti-fascist and anti-imperialist liberation" and of the 13th Romanian Communist Party Congress, as well as the launching, in USA and Mexico, of a book, *Stereospecific Polymerization of Isoprene,* by Comrade Acad. Dr. Eng. Elena Ceauşescu.

The following significant actions were initiated in the field of press: interview of Comrade Nicolae Ceauşescu, president of the Socialist Republic of Romania with the American journalist John Dallach, Washington correspondent of the *Hearst* syndicate; the publication of a large number of favorable articles about our country in the press of Mexico, Costa Rica, Brazil, Colombia, Venezuela, Ecuador etc.

"It should be noted that the image of Romania was better and more widely covered by the Latin American and Canadian press than the American, which continued to publish a number of tendentious articles initiated by circles hostile to our country, focused on problems of human rights, with an emphasis on aspects of religious freedom and the situation of citizens of the Hungarian minority."

Fig. 4. Bucharest, Romanian Ministry of Foreign Affairs, signing an agreement for cultural, educational and scientific exchanges between the Socialist Republic of Romania and the U.S.A, February 18, 1967 (F.O.C.R.).

"The following activities in the period are also worth mentioning: the tour to the United States of the *Madrigal* chorus; visits to the United States of Dinu Giurescu and the film directors Andrei Blaier, Alexandru Tsatsos; the Romanian-American conference on *The Role of Water and Ions in the Functioning of Biologicam Membranes* (Houston, U.S.A.); an international conference organized by the Romanian Commission on Military History and Brooklyn College, New York; the continuation of the Romanian musicians' programs in Venezuela, Ecuador, and Colombia; the activity of the Romanian university chairs in the United States.

"We also underline the positive impact and favorable image of Romania that resulted from Romanian participation in the Summer Olympics in Los Angeles.

"Nevertheless, the cultural and scientific exchanges and efforts to make Romania better known in the countries of the Western Hemisphere have not risen to the potential generated by our party and national foreign policy.

"We underline the fact that, on the one hand, there is no satisfactory link between the cultural-artistic propaganda and the economic, technological and scientific activities, in the sense of using the latter fields to publicize our country's achievements, internal and external, and that, on the other hand, the propagandistic materials produced in Romania are not always adequately attuned to the English and Spanish languages or to the publics they address.

The propaganda activities in culture and press of the Office of Relations V for the year 1985 will focus on the following :

– Present Romania's economic and social achievements, and its prospects of development, based on the documents of the 13th Congress of the Romanian Communist Party;

– Publish volumes from the work of Comrade Nicolae Ceauşescu, president of the Socialist Republic of Romania, of Comrade Acad. Dr. Eng. Elena Ceauşescu, as well as reference materials on Romania;

– Present our people's social-political, economic and cultural stage of development, human rights and liberties, our party and national policies; counter irredentist, chauvinistic propaganda and misrepresentation of Romanian history and realities;

– Commemoration of important events (40 since the victory over Nazi Germany, two decades from the 9th Congress of the Romanian Communist Party, and the International Youth Year).

– A wider distribution of the values of Romanian culture, civilization and spirit."[33]

1985 – "Romania's cultural, technological and scientific relations and propaganda activity in the Western Hemisphere were focused on presenting the economic-social achievements and socialist Romania's prospects for development, in conformity with the resolutions of the 13th Congress of the Romanian Communist Party, publicize information on the Romanian people's life and work, on the development of democracy, the *de facto* observance of fundamental human rights for all citizens, as well as on counteracting revisionist, hostile propaganda and the misrepresentation of Romanian history and reality.

"Special emphasis was laid on popularizing Romania's foreign policy, the position of the country and of President Nicolae Ceauşescu on the major international issues.

"In the propaganda activity the focus was on commemorating, in the countries of the Western Hemisphere, such outstanding events as the 40th anniversary of the victory over Nazi Germany, two decades from the 9th Congress of the Romanian Communist Party, the International Youth Year, as well as on widely promoting in the same area values of Romanian culture, civilization and spirit.

---

[33]A.M.A.E., not catalogued file, "Report of activitate pe anul 1984", No. 5/0638, February 12, 1985, 15 pp, signed Ion Beşteliu, director a.i., pp. 10-12.

Fig. 5. President Nixon's visit to the R.S.R. – welcomed by President Ceaușescu
at the Otopeni airport, 1969 (F.O.C.R.).

"It should be noted that activities in our country's interest in this field in 1985 brought increased success in reaching our policy targets. They directly contributed not only to the general development of the relations between Romania and the United States, Canada and the countries of Latin America; but they also contributed to a better knowledge of Romania's domestic and foreign policies in the respective countries, and in this sense we highlight the following important activities:

a) The opening of the exhibitions *Moments in the Romanian People's Struggle for Independence*, *Contemporary Images of Romania* and *Romania Today* (Peru, Argentina, Brazil, Uruguay, Chile, Ecuador).

b) Organizing Romanian film festivals (Canada, U.S.A., Ecuador, Peru, Venezuela, Brazil, Argentina, Uruguay). Winning the award at the scientific film festival in Sao Paulo.

c) Tours of artistic groups in the U.S.A. and Canada, individual visits by artists in Chile etc. First prize at the International Violin Competition in Chile.

4) Organizing of a Romanian-American history conference at the Romanian Library in New York, and a conference on cellular biology and pathology in Bucharest.

"Nevertheless, the cultural and scientific exchanges have not always reached their full potential as planned by the party and national foreign policy. We note especially the absence of a link between the cultural-artistic propaganda and the economic, technological and scientific activities, i.e. using the latter fields to popularize our country's overall domestic and international achievements. The possibilities offered by the various cultural programs undertaken with countries in the region were not realized due to economic difficulties experienced by some Romanian cultural-artistic companies. Moreover, not all the propaganda materials produced in Romania for these countries by Office of Relations V have met the specific requirements of the targeted public with regard to style and expression in English and Spanish.

"The press, radio and television activities led to some positive results, as follows:

1. The mass media in Canada (press, radio and television) reflected positively on the visit to Canada of Comrade Nicolae Ceauşescu, president of the Socialist Republic of Romania, as well as Romania's international position and general initiatives (i.e. disarmament, the Near East).

2. A wider and more accurate coverage of Romania in the Latin American press, more favorable articles published (Brazil, Mexico, Costa Rica, Colombia, Venezuela).

3. Romanian music and cultural-scientific programs were broadcast on various radio stations in Canada, U.S.A. and in some of the Latin American countries, such as Venezuela and Brazil; the film festival was broadcast on TV in Uruguay.

4. M.A.E., including the Office of Relations V, received the visit of many foreign correspondents from the U.S.A. and from some of the Latin American countries.

5. The Romanian diplomatic missions organized press conferences on the 23rd of August and other occasions which presented Romanian achievements in its domestic development and foreign policy; these were echoed in the press and television.

"It must to be noted, however, that many tendentious articles continued to appear in the United States, at the initiative of circles hostile to our country. These focused on problems concerning human rights, especially referring to religious freedom and the situation of the Romanian citizens of Hungarian ethnicity, as well as to the issue of the Most Favored Nation clause.

"Measures to counteract such activities hostile to our country were taken in cooperation with the Press and Culture Department and several other institutions.

"In 1986 press and culture propaganda activity by Office of Relations V in the two Americas will be directed towards further presenting Romania's economic-social and foreign policy achievements. It will make known Romanian values in culture, civilization and spirit; publish works by Comrade Nicolae Ceauşescu, president of the Socialist Republic of Romania, by Comrade Acad. Dr. Eng. Elena Ceauşescu, first vice-prime minister of the government, as well as reference books on Romanian subjects; and appropriately commemorate the 65th anniversary of the founding of the Romanian Communist Party, as well as the International Year of Peace. More intensive, diversified efforts will be made. The Romanian diplomatic offices in the two Americas will be even more actively involved in countering revisionist, hostile, confrontational and critical propaganda against our country."[34].

1986 – "In 1986 Romanian cultural, technological and scientific relations and propaganda in the two Americas will also be focused on widely publicizing Romanian achievements in the years of socialist construction, and particularly during the past 21 years, when Comrade Nicolae Ceauşescu has been the leader of our party and state. They will also underline the prospects of our country for multilateral development as provided for by the resolutions of the 13th Congress of the Romanian Communist Party; they will present Romania's dynamic, constructive foreign policy and promote the initiatives of world importance launched by Comrade Nicolae Ceauşescu, president of the Romanian Socialist Republic.

"At the same time, special emphasis was laid, in the propaganda activities, on celebrating important Romanian events in the countries of the two Americas. Thus, prestigious political and cultural programs were organized in a very big number of countries under the responsibility of Office of Relations V (Argentina, Brazil, Mexico, Cuba, Colombia, Costa Rica, Canada, U.S.A., Venezuela, Peru) to celebrate the 65th anniversary of the foundation of the Romanian Communist Party, 50 years from the trial in Braşov of the communist and anti-fascist militants, and 42 years from the victory of the anti-fascist and anti-imperialist revolution for social and national liberation. More such activities marked significant events from the history of the Romanian people, of its struggle for liberty, independence and progress.

---

[34]Ibidem, "Report of Activity for 1985" No. 5/0443, February 1986, 19 pp, signed Ion Beşteliu, director a.i., pp. 12-15.

Fig. 6. White House, President Richard Nixon and President Nicolae Ceauşescu,
1970 (F.O.C.R.).

"There was a focus on publishing works by Comrade Nicolae Ceauşescu, president of the Socialist Republic of Romania and by Comrade Acad. Dr. Eng. Elena Ceauşescu. Mention should be made here of the volume *Nicolae Ceauşescu – Romania, Socialism, Democracy, Independence, Peace* published in Venezuela; preparations were also made for the publication of some academic works by Comrade Acad. Dr. Eng. Elena Ceauşescu in Argentina and Brazil.

"Press, radio and television efforts were equally successful, as in the following:

– Comrade President Nicolae Ceauşescu's interview in the Mexican newspaper *Mundo International*.

– Mass media in the United States, Canada and some Latin American countries covered positively the initiative President Ceausescu to establish the 5% unilateral limitation of armament, military equipment and military expenses.

– There was wider and more concrete coverage of Romania in the media of Canada and Latin America, as more articles favorable to our country were published by the press of Brazil, Mexico, Costa Rica, Colombia, Venezuela, Peru and Canada.

– Radio programs of Romanian music and cultural-scientific information were broadcast in Latin America, Canada, U.S.A.

– The Romanian diplomatic missions organized events, including press conferences on the occasion of the 65th anniversary of the founding of the Romanian Communist Party, presenting the Romanian people's success in its development and foreign affairs, similarly on 10 year anniversary of Romania's joining the Group of 77.

"It should be noted, nevertheless, that many tendentious articles were published in the United States, initiated by groups hostile to our country, referring to human rights, particularly to aspects of religious freedom and to the situation of the Romanian citizens of Hungarian ethnicity, as relevant to the Most Favored Nation clause.

"Generally, despite all the positive results, the propaganda efforts in the areas covered by Office of Relations V are still far from reaching the requirements and achieving its full potential. There is a serious contrast between the perception of Romania in the U.S.A. and today's reality of socialist Romania, its position and prestige under President Nicolae Ceauşescu.

"In 1987, the Office of Relations V staff at the department and office level shall focus their propaganda in culture and media in the two Americas on the following efforts:

a) Publishing works by Comrade Nicolae Ceauşescu, president of the Socialist Republic of Romania, and by Comrade Acad. Dr. Eng. Elena Ceauşescu, as well as general reference materials on Romania.

b) Presenting the social, political, economic and cultural levels reached in our people's development, and the human rights and liberties of the Romanian citizens of minority nationality.

c) Countering hostile propaganda that disparages human rights in Romania, revisionist and chauvinistic propaganda and distortions of Romania's history and realities.

d) Commemorating significant events in the history of the Romanian people (110 years from the state's independence and 40 years from the proclamation of the Republic).

e) Applying more efficiently the provisions for cultural-scientific exchanges established with the countries in the two Americas, taking into account Romanian interests in the respective countries.

f) Disseminating widely knowledge of the values of Romanian culture, civilization and spirit.

g) Encouraging the country desks to monitor closely the propaganda activities undertaken by the Romanian diplomatic offices in the area covered; their suggestions and proposals to improve our country's presence in their respective countries."[35].

---

[35] Idem, "Raport de activitate pe anul 1986" nr. 5/0222, 20 January 1987, 17 pp, signed Ion Beşteliu, director a.i., pp. 12-15.

Fig. 7. President Ceauşescu receives a group of American students on a visit to the R.S.R. under the "Friendship Ambassadors" program, 1974 (F.O.C.R.).

"In 1987 Romania's cultural, technological and scientific relations and propaganda in the two Americas focused on presenting Socialist Romania's economic and social achievements as well as her prospects for future of development, based on the resolutions of the 13th Congress of the Romanian Communist Party. There was as well a focus on making known the living and working conditions of the Romanian people, the development of our democracy with its fundamental and genuine human rights and freedoms for all the country's citizens. Also attention focused on opposing the reactionary, revisionist, hostile and distorted propaganda concerning Romanian history and reality.

"Special emphasis was laid on making known our country's dynamic and constructive international policy, the initiatives of considerable world importance of Comrade President Nicolae Ceauşescu concerning the main international issues.

"Propaganda highlighted the work and resolutions of the National Conference of the Romanian Communist Party; the 110th anniversary of Romania's independence and the 40th anniversary of the founding of the Republic; and other significant events in the history of the Romanian people, in its struggle for liberty, independence and progress and disseminated widely information on the values of Romanian culture, civilization and spirit throughout the countries of the two Americas.

"A permanent target was the publication of works by Comrade President Nicolae Ceauşescu. Mention should be made, in this connection of the volume *Nicolae Ceauşescu: Fundamental Issues Today: Abolishing Underdevelopment and the Construction of a New Economic World Order*, published in Argentina.

"One may conclude that activity in this field in 1987 served well the goals of Romanian policy and our country's interests and directly contributed not only to the general development of Romania's relations with the U.S.A., Canada and the Latin American countries, but also to increase awareness of Romania's internal and external policies in these. There were:

Important initiatives in the press, such as: Comrade President Nicolae Ceauşescu's interview in the Mexican newspaper *El sol de Mexico*; publication of a supplement devoted to Romania in the Chilean newspaper *El Mercurio*; publication of *The Romanian People: A Permanent Latin Presence in Eastern Europe* and *Romania: Development, Cooperation, Peace* in the Brazilian weekly *Flashes Nacionais o Internacionais*; as well as many favorable articles on Romania published in Argentina, Brazil, Canada, Costa Rica, Chile, Peru, Venezuela, Uruguay, Cuba.

b) Romanian historians participated in annual conventions of American historians and conferences at various American universities; the complete article *The Deliberate Falsification of Romania's History by the Hungarian Academy of Science* was published in the Argentinian journal *Historia* nr. 27/87.

c) Days of Romanian culture were organized in Argentina and Canada; a Festival of Romanian Film in Argentina; Romanian documentaries shown in Argentina, Brazil, Chile, Mexico, U.S.A.; book exhibitions, primarily featuring works by Comrade President Nicolae Ceauşescu and by Comrade Elena Ceauşescu in Argentina, Costa Rica, Canada, Mexico, U.S.A., Brazil; photography and documentary exhibitions U.S.A., Brazil, Mexico, Costa Rica, Canada, Chile, Argentina, Cuba, Peru; festive reunions in Cuba.

d) Programs of Romanian music, culture and science in various radio broadcasts in Latin America, Canada and U.S.A.

"At the same time, however, many tendentious articles continued to appear in the American press, produced by groups hostile to our country, focused on human rights, especially aspects of religious freedom and the situation of the Romanian citizens of Hungarian ethnicity, as well as on the Most Favored Nation clause governing commercial relations with the United States.

"Generally, all the positive results, the cultural-scientific exchanges and the propaganda still did not always reach the full potential of the foreign policy of our party and state or the prestige of Comrade President Nicolae Ceauşescu. Furthermore, on one hand the possibilities offered by the various cultural agreements and programs agreed upon with the countries of the region have not been realized, and, on the other hand not all the propaganda materials produced in Romania have met the expectations of the target audiences in the countries for which the Office of Relations V is responsible, in so far as English and Spanish style is concerned.

Fig. 8. The White House, President Nicolae Ceauşescu's visit
to the United States at the invitation of President Carter, 1978 (F.O.C.R.).

"The Office of Relations V and the Romanian diplomatic posts in the area concerned shall emphasize the following in their future activity:

– Publishing works by Comrade President Nicolae Ceauşescu and Comrade Acad. Dr. Eng. Elena Ceauşescu, first vice-prime minister of the Government.

– Publishing reference materials on Romania.

– Commemorate fully the 70th anniversary of the foundation of the unified Romanian nation state.

– Presenting the social, political, economic and cultural aspects of our people's development, and the human rights and freedoms of the Romanian citizens of differing ethnicities.

– Confront the hostile propaganda that denigrates our record on human rights and the reactionary and chauvinistic propaganda which misrepresents Romania's history and realities.

– Disseminate widely information about the values of Romanian culture, civilization and spirit.

– Increase control by the appropriate offices of propaganda activities undertaken by the Romanian diplomatic posts in the relevant countries and focus attention on suggestions and proposals for the improving Romania's image in the respective countries.

– Finalize the negotiations for cultural exchanges with Argentina and Colombia as well as the Memorandum of Agreement with Canada for cultural, academic and athletic exchanges."[36].

At the beginning of 1988, close to the overthrow of the totalitarian regime, Bucharest still preferred to revoke unilaterally the Most Favored Nation clause with the United States, rather than easing the internal repression. By then there had been repeated proposals in both houses of the American Congress to suspend the clause for Romania, and the prospect of its renewal was slim.

---

[36]Idem, "Raport de activitate pe anul 1987" nr. 5/0255, 13 January 1988, 21 pp, signed Ion Beşteliu, director a.i., pp. 14-17.

Fig. 9. Moscow, meeting between N. Ceauşescu, general secretary of the Romanian Communist Party and M. Gorbachev, general secretary of the C.C. of the C.P.S.U., 1985 (F.O.C.R.).

It was due, to a great extent, to the American Embassy in Bucharest, led with some interruptions by ambassadors David B. Funderburk[37] and

---

[37]D. B. Funderburk –Fulbright scholar in Romania (1970), U.S.I.A. researcher in Romania (1975), professor of history at the Campbell University, North Carolina (1976-1981). Appointed ambassador to Romania on October 2, 1981; his resignation from the post was accepted on April 29, 1985. See David B. Funderburk, *Pinstripes and Reds: An American Ambassador Caught Between the State Department & the Romanian Communists, 1981–1985* (Washington DC: Selous Foundation Press, 1987)

Roger Kirk[38], that Washington was able to know the true situation of Romania over the last decade of its dictatorial system, the nature and mechanisms of that society; and that attempts were made to normalize the bilateral relations in spite of all odds. One of the diplomats on the team of both ambassadors was Ernest Hargreaves Latham Jr., whose responsibility were the bilateral cultural relations. He is one of the four members of the American diplomatic mission whom Funderburk relied on in representing his country, and "who "assisted me and did much of the work in finding out the truth about the Romanian regime and Soviet-Romanian relations."[39]

Vadim Guzun

---

[38]R. Kirk – career diplomat, he served with the American diplomatic missions in Rome, Moscow (twice), New Delhi, Saigon, he was ambassador in Somalia (1973-1975) and UN ambassador in Viena (1978-1983), deputy assistant secretary of state for international organizations (1983-1985). He was appointed ambassador to Romania on November 15, 1985, where he served until July 5, 1989. Edward J. Derwinski, counselor of the State Department, seems to have stated, during a meeting with Aurel Duma, the Romanian minister-secretary of state, on May 27, 1986, that "the style of the new American ambassador, different from his predecessor's, is more favourable for attaining agreements between Romania and the United States.", A.M.A.E., *S.U.A.*/1986, file 1082, p. 58, note of the Office of Relations V to Minister Ilie Văduva, May 30, 1986. See also Roger Kirk, Mircea Răceanu, *Romania versus the United States: Diplomacy of the Absurd, 1985-1989* (New York: St. Martin's Press, 1994).

[39]David B. Funderburk, *Pinstripes and Reds..., op. cit.*, p. vii. The other three diplomats mentioned by the author are his Deputy Chief of Mission Frank Corry, the military attaché Franklin Mastro and the press attaché William Edwards.

Documents

MINISTERUL DE INTERNE
Unitatea *3H/MA.*

Fi 230990 v 1
LATHAM
ERNEST -
HARGRAVES
11. 08. 1938
Ow -83.

DOSAR DE URMĂRIRE INFORMATIVĂ Nr. *15052*

privind pe „*LASCU*"
(nume conspirativ)

VOL I

Deschis la data de *23. 09. 1983*

Închis la data de _____

Cover of Ernest H. Latham's Securitate file
opened on September 23, 1983

Telegram of the R.S.R. Embassy in the F.R.G.,
to the M.F.A. Headquarters, concerning granting a diplomatic visa to Ernest Latham, for the
purpose of travelling to Romania

Ministry of Foreign Affairs   Secret
West Berlin/020598/09.25.1979/22.00

TELEGRAM

The American Military Mission in West Berlin is kindly asking for a diplomatic visa for collaborator ERNEST H. LATHAM, born on August 11, 1938, holder of diplomatic passport no. x120426.

At the same time, it is asking, if possible, for a diplomatic visa for the wife of the above-mentioned, holder of a usual simple passport no. z2842722. Her name is KAREN E. JAEHNE LATHAM, born on September 2, 1948, in the U.S.A.

They intend to travel in the period October 5th to the 21st. Their travel is of both an official and private nature, after visiting the U.S. Embassy, they want to spend about ten days in Romania to visit a few touristic areas.

Kindly provide your answer,

M. UNGUREANU

A.N.C.S.S.A., *Informative* fund, file no. 1093922, vol. I, p. 11.
Resolution: "Steps for surveillance. Complex. / Lt. Col., SIG, undecipherable / 10.04.1979".

-2-

Communication to the 3rd Directorate within D.S.S., to Bureau III within the County Inspectorate Suceava of the Ministry of Internal Affairs, regarding the visit of the diplomat Ernest Latham to this county, pointing out he belongs among the "cadre of the C.I.A." and requesting measures of informative surveillance

Ministry of Internal Affairs

Department of State Security   Top Secret

3rd Directorate   Unique copy

No. 312/MA/D/00128606/10.10.1979

TELEX

To the County Inspectorate Suceava

of the Ministry of Internal Affairs

Bureau III

Within the period 10.11 to 20, CY, the American citizen ERNEST H. LATHAM, born on August 11, 1938, will travel to Suceava. He is accompanied by his wife, KAREN LATHAM, born on September 2, 1948, in the U.S.A.

ERNEST H. LATHAM belongs to the American Military Mission in West Berlin and, according to our information, is employed by the C.I.A.

The stated goal of his travel to Suceava is to visit the monasteries.

Please take the measures for informative surveillance of the LATHAM couple and communicate to us the outcomes.

Deputy Chief of Directorate

Colonel, SIG, IONESCU VIRGILIU

A.N.C.S.S.A., *Informative* fund, file no. 1093922, vol. I, p. 14.
Handwritten indications: 1) "GELU"; 2) "10.10.1979 / Was transmitted
according to address. / SIG, undecipherable".

-3-

Note by informer "Ivan" regarding the arrival
of diplomat Ernest Latham and wife to R.S.R.;
schedule of the Latham couple in Bucharest,
proceedings for intelligence surveillance

312/LV   Top Secret

Source "IVAN"   Unique copy

"Rozalia" House   10.11.1979

NOTE

Friday, 10.06., CY the LATHAMs arrived in the R.S.R., by plane,
from the F.R.G. He is a cultural and press attaché at the U.S. Embassy in
the F.R.G. and a good friend of GARNETT.

Nevertheless, upon arrival, GARNETT did not want to receive him,
indicating he was ill (which was not the case).

On Monday, they said they had visited the Village Museum and
eaten at Athenée Palace.

Monday, IONESCU I. accompanied them to the Cinema magazine,
where they talked to MIRCEA ALEXANDRESCU and to Buftea, where
they talked to PIVNICERU and DOINA MARTA about Romanian

cinematography. Also on Monday, they had dinner at "Capşa", inviting IONESCU as well.

They left the impression of knowing the city well, although they did not appear to have been here before. It is not known what they did on Tuesday and Wednesday morning.

At lunch, they were invited to "Capşa" by GARNETT. STRAIN and IONESCU also participated.

During dinner, he discussed with IONESCU Romanian cinematography and said he would like to write a book on the subject. He wanted to come to the R.S.R. for 6 to 8 months. He discussed extensively with STRAIN and GARNETT. He complained that they had quite a hard time in the F.R.G. He explained that a secretary at the U.S Embassy wanting to put some files in order, had also burnt some special documents.

On Thursday evening, they leave for Suceava, to return on Tuesday, when they want to see several Romanian movies and organize a roundtable at the Library (Thursday), inviting S. NICOLAESCU, GĂITAN V., and DANELIUC. The entire program is organized by I. IONESCU, who is not aware of the true purpose of the couple's visit.

One day, I. FERGUSON was given a call by a certain LUCIAN, from Bucharest, who seems to be a friend of his.

"IVAN"

N.B.

From the data we have, it looks like LATHAM ERNEST is actually a press attaché at the Military Mission of the U.S. in F.R. Germany. This information is derived from his request for the grant of a visa to enter the S.R. of Romania, which states this affiliation, and from the fact that, after his visit to the U.S. Embassy in Bucharest, the above-mentioned wishes to stay for approximately ten more days in order to visit a few tourist areas.

The meeting LATHAM ERNEST had at "Capşa" restaurant with MORRIS GARNETT, counselor for press and culture, and STEPHEN STRAIN, press attaché, was also surveilled by the I.D.B.T. source.

On 10.11.1979, LATHAM ERNEST and wife left for Suceava, where they will stay until 10.14.1979, when they will return to Bucharest. The county has been informed in order to take steps for control, the more so as they intend to rent a car without a driver.

Measures will be taken through source "IVAN" so that the round table with the three filmmakers nominated by LATHAM ERNEST's wife should not take place at the American Library, but at the working place of the respective Romanian citizens, where standard control measures will be taken.

MJR ILIE GHEORGHE

A.N.C.S.S.A., *Informative* fund, file no. 1093922, vol. I, ff. 15-16.
Resolution: "The source will inform us in due course about the events organized for the LATHAM couple. The source will continue to take into consideration FERGUSON's capture and his connections. / CPT LAZĂR VALERIU".

-4-

Note by MB 0672/Bucharest to the 3rd Directorate within D.S.S., regarding the shadowing of targets "Gelu", "Stan" and "Licu" – Ernest Latham, carried out on October 10, 1979

Ministry of Internal Affairs	Top Secret
Department of State Security	Unique copy
MB 0672 / Buch.	
No. 12/D/00362890 of 10.15.1979	

To the 3rd Directorate / Ind. 312

NOTE REGARDING SHADOWING OF TARGET "GELU", CARRIED OUT ON 10.10.1979

Following your request no. 00145694 we communicate to you the following:

Activity of the target

At 10.00 "GELU" was taken under surveillance while he was at work.

From his office (Consulate) "GELU" left at 12.40, together with "STAN" and ERNEST LATHAM ("LICU") and wife and walked to the "București" restaurant*, arriving at 13.50. This location afforded the opportunity to carry out special measures.

They all left the restaurant at 15.20 and walked to the U.S. Consulate, which they reached at 15.30. Here, the shadowing of "GELU" was ended in favor of the target "LICU".

Surveillance finished.

Commander of the Unit, SIG, undecipherable

f. Bureau Chief, Lt. Col., SIG, undecipherable**

R.D.001/1049/11.10.1979
A.N.C.S.S.A., *Informative* fund, file no. 1093922, vol. I, p. 31.
Handwritten indication at the beginning of the document: "B.2/M.A.".
* Underlined here and in the rest of the document.
** The seal of the military base was also applied.

-5-

Note by the County Inspectorate Suceava of Ministry of the Internal Affairs, to the 3rd Directorate within D.S.S., regarding the recordings of Ernest Latham's conversations with his wife on October 11 and 12, 1979; conclusion – "none of them had a great night"

Ministry of Internal Affairs	Top Secret
County Inspectorate Suceava	Copy no. 1
No. 3/V.T./002871 of 11.07.1979	

To the Ministry of Internal Affairs / 3rd Directorate – Bureau I

Following your telegraphic order no. 312/M.A./00128606 of 10.10.1979, as well as the telephone reporting on 10.13.1979, we report that in the period October 11-12, C.Y, the American citizen ERNEST LATHAM ("EREMIA"), from the American Military Mission in West Berlin, and his wife KAREN LATHAM, were present on the territory of our county.

Out of the information and operative steps undertaken in order to find out the activities, behavior, and connections of the above mentioned it became clear that "EREMIA" was interested to know Romania's policy. There were no other data of interest to the Securitate bodies.

Find attached the note "T" no. 007551 of 10.19.1979 regarding the talks carried out by the target at the site of his accommodation.

Chief of the County Securitate

Colonel, SIG, RANGU CONSTANTIN

Chief of Bureau III, Colonel, SIG, FURTUNĂ NICOLAE

[Annex]

Translated from English	Top Secret
No. post: 11 / No. file: 1	Unique copy

No. 007551/1

Date: 10.19.1979 "EREMIA" / Hotel "Arcaşul"

Serv. III/V.T.   Tape no. 986 / Room 204

[NOTE]

20.23. While listening to music, they discuss a few issues that are of no special importance (about the items they intend to buy from the "Shop", what they would like to have for dinner).

Referring to the program of the next day, they know nothing for sure. "Everything - as the target lady says – depends on the weather."

At 20.58, they left the room, to return at 22.50. No more dialogue.

10.12.1979

06.10. Looks like none had a great night (she recounts her nightmare). The target lady blames it on the book she had read the previous night. At a certain moment, the target lady looks into a publication on Romania. He asks her: "Is there anything about Romania's policy? This is interesting!"*

Then they listened to a radio station broadcasting in English (at the beginning, there was a health bulletin, then the latest news on the international political situation, followed by sports news).

At 10.20 they left the room.

On October 13 and 14, 1979, there was no conversation in the room.

10.19.1979

Translated, SIG, undecipherable

A.N.C.S.S.A., *Informative* fund, file no. 1093922, vol. I, p. 17;
vol. IV, p. 2.
*Underlined in the document.
Resolution: "09.10.1979 / To be exploited. / Col., SIG, undecipherable".

-6-

Note concerning the expected arrival of Ernest Latham as a diplomat in the R.S.R.; data regarding the life and activity of the diplomat, considered to be "employed by the C.I.A.", "special measures for the surveillance of his activity"

311/M.A.   Top Secret

Unique copy

04.07.1983

NOTE

According to our information, the diplomat ERNEST H. LATHAM*, born on 08.11.1938 in the U.S.A., will join the U.S. Embassy in the R.S.R. as a cultural attaché in July C.Y. He is married to KAREN JAEHNE LATHAM, born on 09.02.1948 in the U.S.A.

The LATHAMs have visited our country in the period 11 to 20 October 1979, and were housed in the residence of an American diplomat, on 124 Eminescu Street, who at the time was out of the country.

At that time, the diplomat ERNEST LATHAM was working at the American Military Mission in West Berlin, having a diplomatic passport. Although his wife was not employed by the Department of State, she had a diplomatic passport.

During his stay in the country, he was the responsibility of the diplomat "ZAMFIR", employed by the C.I.A., who made efforts to give the visit an unofficial aspect, and organized for the LATHAMs, besides visits to the embassy, a 4-day trip to the monasteries in Moldavia.

The information and operative proceedings carried out on him have brought the following results:

During the time mentioned above, the diplomat and his wife resided in a villa in Berlin, one of the villas taken over by the Americans ever since 1945. LATHAM was a neighbor of the American consul – the highest American resident in the F.R.G., who had the rank of a Major General, in fact was a "coroner" (sic., possibly 'Colonel'), as this rank used to be called once upon a time in the U.S.A.

LATHAM operated in Athens and, from there, he was acting Director of the Press Bureau in Beirut, in charge with the Voice of America in Lebanon and the neighboring countries.

LATHAM's direct boss was ROWEN, who worked not in Athens, but Helsinki. ROWEN became chief of the Agency in Washington immediately after leaving Helsinki. (There was no direct reference as to the agency.)

For medical examinations, treatment, or hospitalizations, LATHAM and wife went to the American Military Hospital in Wiesbaden, the hospital of the American occupation forces in the F.R.G.

LATHAM disclosed to the American cultural counsellor at the time that, before leaving the F.R.G. for his visit to our country, the director of the "Voice of America" visited him in Berlin.

The American diplomat also asserted that one of his secretaries in Berlin, ISABELE RORSE, had worked in Rome for many years on very important secret files, to which a very limited number of Americans had access.

The diplomat mentioned that, ever since that period and even a long time previously, both he and his wife had started taking Romanian language lessons at the Romanian studies program of Rochester University, in the U.S.A.

While in Bucharest and at the monasteries in Northern Moldova, LATHAM took pictures of many tourism sites (monasteries, churches, and cultural establishments). Nevertheless, in Bucharest he used, on several occasions, routes that had absolutely no connection to his visit.

Both in Bucharest and in the province, LATHAM used methods and means of self-checking in order to discover whether he was being shadowed.

Also worth noting is the fact that, while the diplomat "ZAMFIR", employed by the C.I.A., paid the utmost attention to LATHAM's visit to Romania, the American cultural counsellor at that time, MORRIS GARNETT, gave no importance to it, even suggesting that LATHAM's presence was inopportune for him.

One day, when he was supposed to accompany the LATHAMs on a tour of the capital, GARNETT asked his Romanian driver to handle this for him.

N.O.

The above data, as well as other materials show that ERNEST LATHAM is employed by the C.I.A., and, as a result, we will have to take outstanding surveillance measures of his activity during the time he will be posted in our country.

Lt. Col., SIG, undecipherable

A.N.C.S.S.A., *Informative* fund, file no. 1093922, vol. I, ff. 75-76.
*Here and further on underlined in the document.
Resolution: "Keep on file", followed by handwritten indication: "Filed/R.".

-7-

Action plan of the 3rd Directorate within D.S.S. for the Information Surveillance Dossier regarding the diplomat Ernest Latham, who was introduced to his post at the Press and Cultural Section of the U.S. Embassy in Bucharest on September 9, 1983, "suspected to be employed by the C.I.A. with the mission to gather information in the socio-political and military fields".

311/M.A.   Top Secret

Unique copy

10.09.1983

Approved,

Lt. Col., SIG, undecipherable

ACTION PLAN

ON I.S.D. "LASCU" CONDUCTED UPON AMERICAN DIPLOMAT LATHAM ERNEST HARGREAVES

On 09.09.1983, the American diplomat LATHAM ERNEST HARGREAVES, born on 08.11.1938, in Massachusetts – U.S.A., assumed his post at the Cultural Section of the U.S. Embassy in Bucharest. He will fill the position of cultural attaché, replacing diplomat VICTOR JACKOVICH, who left the position. He is married to KAREN JAEHNE LATHAM, born on 09.02.1948, in the U.S. The LATHAMs have visited our country before in the period 11 to 20 October 1979, and in charge of their visit was the diplomat "ZAMFIR", employed by the C.I.A.

ERNEST LATHAM graduated Dartmouth College in the U.S.A. in the year 1960, after which he joined the U.S. Army, and has the rank of lieutenant.

In 1966, he earned a doctoral degree at Roosevelt University, after which, in August of the same year, he was hired by U.S.I.A. as a trainee.

After completing an Arabic language study program, he was appointed a deputy attaché in Beirut, within the Cultural Section.

From 1970 to 1973, he served as an assistant press and culture attaché in Vienna, then he was called back to Washington, where he took classes in the Greek language. In 1974, he was appointed cultural attaché in Nicosia. He worked there until 1977, when he returned to headquarters. From 1977 to 1979, he followed a language training course there, and he was then sent to the Military Mission in West Berlin.

According to the information we have from the operative surveillance conducted during his visit to our country in 1979, as well as building on the experience acquired by the surveillance of cultural attachés preceding him, we conclude that LATHAM ERNEST is likely employed by the C.I.A. for the purpose of gathering information on socio-political and military subjects.

Taking into consideration the above and with the aim of averting a leak of information, as well as in order to document and unmask the diplomat's spying activity carried out against our country, I suggest for the following information and operative measures to be approved:

[YES]* 1) Steering with diversified tasks in the proximity of the diplomat of the informer "RODICA", who works directly with him in order to carry out his official work assignments.

Deadline: permanent

In charge: Lt. Col. MILITARU A.

[YES] 2) Giving priority to the surveillance of contacts made by the diplomat at educational and cultural institutions in the capital. We will take into consideration the doubtful contacts made by the diplomat with Romanian citizens who are holders of secrets or who have benefitted from exchanges with the U.S.A.** In this respect, the sources "MITU" and "CEZAR" will be taken into consideration.

Deadline: permanent

In charge: Lt. Col. MILITARU A.

3) Concentrating on "work on" or, from case to case, "study on" *lecturers, PhD candidates and especially American students who come* into *contact more often* with the diplomat under circumstances making them suspected of collecting and delivering information.

Deadline: permanent for "work on" cases

In charge: Lt. Col. MILITARU A.

4) Using security means in order to catch the diplomat within the system of impersonal connections within the agency among Romanian citizens.

Deadline: permanent

In charge: Lt. Col. MILITARU A.

[NO] 5) Via the informers "RICĂ" and "BINDEA", I will obtain duplicate keys from "LASCU"'s house and car, for the purpose of secretly penetrating into his residence, in order to study the possibilities to introduce T.O. means.

Deadline: 01.12.1983

In charge: Lt. Col. MILITARU A.

[YES] 6) Finding out and controlling by specific security means the conversations the diplomat carries out in public places, in and outside Bucharest, with Romanian citizens who are suspected of treason.

Deadline: permanent

In charge: Lt. Col. MILITARU A.

[YES] 7) Preparing and controlling, with specific security measures, all the diplomat's travels throughout the territory, pressing especially for finding the organization of some Romanian citizens or of those using impersonal communication.

Deadline: permanent

In charge: Lt. Col. MILITARU A.

[Who is "ALBU"?] 8) Initiating operative games with the diplomat through an informer "ALBU", who was introduced to him in a special way by the diplomat "BIANCA". I am going to construct operative games with "ALBU", which should finally lead to his being recruited by the diplomat or by another C.I.A. agent, at "LASCU"'s indication.

Deadline: depending on operative circumstances

In charge: Lt. Col. MILITARU A.

9) I will initiate operations for disinforming and influencing the diplomat via the sources "GRUIA" and "MITU", in collaboration with Bureau "D".

Deadline: permanent

In charge: Lt. Col. MILITARU A.

In February 1984, the action will be analyzed by the chief of the bureau and, taking into consideration the relevant aspects and the results achieved in the surveillance of the diplomat, and the action plan will be supplemented with new tasks, aimed at preventing the leak of information to the diplomat and exposing the spying activities carried out by "LASCU" against our country.

Specialist officer III,

Lt. Col. MILITARU ALEX.

A.N.C.S.S.A., *Informative* fund, file no. 1093922, vol. I, ff. 1-3.
*Here and further down in the document the point by point decision of the superior in the hierarchy.

**Here and further underlined in the document. Final resolution: "1) Select from the Directorate several informers of Arab, Greek origins, whom, based on plans, to infiltrate in the diplomat's intimacy. / 2) Check in all places where he was a diplomat what Romanian diplomats were there simultaneously with him, same for specialists, PhD candidates, other Romania cooperators in the respective countries. This in order to select suspects and agency recruitment for infiltration. *This work style has to be predominant* in action in parallel with initiating measures to compromise the diplomat, to create conditions to act against him. Such aspects should be added to the action plan within the next three months. / Lt. Col., SIG, undecipherable / September 20, 1983".

-8-

D.S.S. report on basis of the account of the informer "Darius", regarding his participation in a reception and his conversation with Ernest Latham; "the adequate answers" of the informer to the cultural attaché's questions on historical matters; "according to the performed training"

311/N.S.   Top Secret

"DARIUS"   23.09.1983

F.N./00115

REPORT

The source had a talk with the new cultural attaché at the U.S. Embassy in Bucharest, ERNEST LATHAM, during the reception offered by MERRY BLOCKER on September 22, CY.

He was interested to know the opinion of a specialist in this field concerning the following subjects:

– if history may or may not be written objectively;

– the way historical facts are interpreted and reinterpreted by each generation;

– what was the role played by the working people in Romania in the interwar period; data regarding the strikes at the Grivița works in 1933;

– generalities regarding the history of arts and the beginnings of secular painting in Romania.

The source provided adequate answers to all these questions. ERNEST LATHAM expressed his wish to continue the conversation on these themes.

The material was delivered according to the performed training. It is exploited at 311/M.A.

SIG, undecipherable

A.N.C.S.S.A., *Informative* fund, file no. 1093922, vol. I, p. 77.
Handwritten indication at the beginning of the document: "V./R.".

-9-

Note by informer "Rodica" regarding activities organized by the Press and Culture Section of the U.S. Embassy in Bucharest

Inf. "RODICA"	Top Secret
House: "Continental"	Unique copy
File 371/1972 / Register: 469	10.18.1983

NOTE

J. SNYDER, a researcher specialized in international security and disarmament at the "Woodrow Wilson" Center in Washington, will arrive in Bucharest Wednesday, October 19, at 15.35, from Frankfurt. He will stay at "Continental" hotel.

On Thursday, Oct. 20, 9.00 a.m., a discussion will be held at the political section, possibly with CORRY and STRECHAN*. At 11.30, a meeting is scheduled at A.D.I.R.I., with a few specialists in disarmament. In the afternoon, at 6.00 p.m., he will hold a conference at the American Library.

On the second day, Friday, Oct. 21, he will go to the Institute of Political Science, for a meeting and talks. Subjects to be tackled, among others, relations between the U.S. and European countries after the I.N.F. negotiations and the transfer of technology, and the relations between European countries and N.A.T.O.

At 13.00 there will be a lunch at the American Library, offered by EDWARDS, followed by discussions. Following were invited: Prof. DUCULESCU, SERGIU VERONA, CONST. MIRCEA NICO-LAESCU, FOTINO, ROȘIANU, CAMELIA BOGDAN, Col. GROZEA, ADRIAN NĂSTASE, MIRCEA MAREȘ, MAGDA CERCELESCU, STELIAN TURDA, ROMAN MOLDOVAN from the Acad. of Social and Political Sciences. From the Embassy: McBRIDE, CONNY, SULLIVAN, MORGAN.

On Saturday, Oct. 22, at 9.35, he leaves for Paris.

A few excerpts from SNYDER's political articles, as well as his bio-bibliographical presentation were sent. Photocopies were sent to the institutions he will visit, as well as to the lunch participants.

Note

We will carry out intelligence surveillance of SNYDER's activity during the entire period of his stay in Bucharest.

Lt. Col., SIG, undecipherable

A.N.C.S.S.A., *Informative* fund, file no. 1093922, vol. I, p. 89.
Handwritten indication at the beginning of document: "LASCU".
* Here and further down underlined in the document.

-10-

Note by D.S.S., based on the accounts of informer "Cezar", regarding the visit of U.S.I.A. inspector Anne Marie Malcock, accompanied by Ernest Latham, to the Ministry of Education; the situation of English language lectureships in the R.S.R., Malcock – why does the Ministry of Education not observe the program of exchanges of lecturers and PhD candidates with the U.S.A.?

311/M.A.	Top Secret
Source: "CEZAR"	Unique copy
File*/ Register**	10.24.1983

NOTE

During the meeting on 10.24.1983, source "CEZAR" reported the following:

On 10.22. C.Y., American diplomat ERNEST LATHAM, accompanying American U.S.I.A. inspector ANNE MARIE MALCOCK, paid a protocol visit to the Ministry of Education. She came to our country to examine the way American lecturers of English language carry out their activity in our country.

During the talks, Mrs. MALCOCK expressed her thanks for the opportunity to visit the American lecturers of English language in Craiova and Timișoara, then asked the following questions:

– Taking into consideration the very recent visit to our country made by GEORGE BUSH and U.S. Secretary of State for Commerce, MALCOLM BALDRIGE, are there wider perspectives for enhancing the volume of cultural exchanges between the R.S.R. and the U.S.A., and especially for exchanges of lecturers and PhD candidates in various fields of activity?

Mrs. MALCOCK asked if, following the increase of foreign trade with the U.S., Romanians would not need two lectureships of English language at the Academy of Economic Sciences as well? She was answered that we have very well trained staff for the A.S.E. students, each of whom studies two or three foreign languages.

– MALCOCK asked how many institutions of higher education there are in the country and how many of them have English language chairs.

– What is the number of students included in the system of English language learning?

– What are the reasons for raising the idea of abolishing the Chair of English Language at the Institute of Higher Education in Constanța?

– Mrs. MALCOCK considers that the city of Constanța, having such intense trade exchanges, should have more graduates in English language.

– Mrs. MALCOCK also inquired why the Ministry of Education never fulfills the program for lecturers and PhD candidates exchanges with the United States of America.

– Has the Ministry of Education had issues of a professional or disciplinary nature with the American lecturers and PhD candidates?

– Does the Ministry of Education consider it necessary to increase the number of American lecturers and PhD candidates in Romania for the academic year 1984-1985? It may do so during the meetings to take place in November in order to negotiate the overall program of cultural exchanges between the R.S.R. and the U.S.A.

– Mrs. MALCOCK inquired, at the same time, about the other foreign language lectureships in Bucharest and the province: how many there are, what are the languages taught in, how many students take the respective lectureship courses, what didactic materials are they using, if they have specialized equipment for teaching the respective languages, and if the ministry has organized exchanges of experience among the foreign and Romanian lecturers?

The meeting lasted one hour and a half. Cultural attaché ERNEST LATHAM did not participate in the talks. On the other hand, upon departure, he insisted for the source to repeat his exact name (probably in order to spell it correctly in the subsequent report).

The source appropriately answered all the problems and questions raised by Mrs. MALCOCK. Another official in the Protocol of the Ministry of Education participated in the meeting.

N.O.

The source was again instructed to follow all aspects pertaining to his contacts with American diplomats, especially with JAMES MORGAN, who will be in charge of the grants for American lecturers and PhD candidates.

Lt. Col., SIG, undecipherable

A.N.C.S.S.A., *Informative* fund, file no. 1093922, vol. I, p. 92.
Handwritten indication at the beginning of document: "LASCU".
* Rubric left blank.
** Rubric left blank.

-11-

Transcript of the recording of a conversation of Ernest Latham's with a colleague within U.S.I.A., performed by the Department of State Security; he - "Ceaușescu manages to get along by doing "somersaults" and other acrobatics, but the regime is as repressive and terrifying as the one in the U.S.S.R."; she - "queues - the most depressive sight"

11.05.1983

SPECIAL OPERATION
LATHAM + INVITED LADY

LATHAM: I guess the English are quite angry. The BBC announced the Canadians...* had not seen the American troops. They played it straight, they were open.

W.: ...

LATHAM: They proceeded exactly like JOHNSON when he intervened in the Dominican Republic.

W.: Yes! At least they had some sort of democratic elections. Very busy now, with the elections, going from one city to the next. (Silences)

W.: To what extent is the ambassador's presence felt around here? I didn't get much of an impression, so far.

L.: He is not very alert, you're right.

W.: I have a hunch he's intensively supported by U.S.I.A.

L.: Something of the sort!

W.: Approximately the same as with HARRIMAN and ERWIN HERBERT.

L.: Oh!

W.: HERBERT works in Bucharest.

L.: HERBERT's wife is a professor.

(Silence)

L.: I was a little bit surprised by the cooperation program.

W.: JESSIE** made it. I was in charge of the program with China.

L.: Do you think we could better accomplish another program?

W.: No, no! The conservatives have become a little too radical. I can't see them pleasing JESSIE now. JESSIE made a rather tough tax program.

L.: I understand HOLMES is now on the "waiting list".

W.: Ahem! He is a very smart person.

L.: I wonder how many people REAGAN will have now, after all these, in this race.

W.: He will have as many as he can keep. What do you mean?

L.: No, I mean how many will be of real help to him.

W.: Now I see. This cannot be predicted. Here it is not like in Europe: full loyalty in the ranks of the party, parliamentary system.

L.: How will things really work out? REAGAN running for presidency and BUSH again for vice-presidency?

W.: Yes. The same. If the economy had not decayed so badly, REAGAN would not have been in the situation he is now. It is really hard to predict what comes next, nevertheless...

L.: Yes, yes.

W.: Are you really interested in politics?

L.: Only in circumstances such as this one. (laughs) ***

W.: I grew up in a family with strong Republican ties. Both my parents were very active along this line.

L.: I very much like the Salt Lake area, I am thinking of making myself a residence there. My parents had a house there.

W.: Have you seen your daughter lately? Are you going to build the house in her name?

L.: No, no. My wife mapped her own path, and so did I. There is no longer understanding between us. She of course cut herself the lion's share from everything. She was an eccentric lady. Nothing was for her. Family was not for her, marriage was not for her, my career did not matter to her, she was unable to set solid family bonds.

W.: Did she travel a lot?

L.: Yes, quite a lot and I think she will always travel. It is very good.

W.: This place is rather crowded, don't you think?

L.: Yes, seems that this is the best restaurant here. *I can't tell you now, but I am going to tell you at the embassy how they manage* best with... (and makes a sign or shows something to her)

W.: Ah! This is interesting! (laughs)

L.: Do you have family? Children, someone?

W.: No, only mother, father and a sister.

L.: In Tennessee?

W.: My sister lives in Washington. My parents divorced when I was four. We weren't together much. I was in high school when she was a student and there has always been an abyss between us. She is doing very well in Washington. She is married, our mother and her husband were old acquaintances. After their marriage, her husband was sent to the "Eastern Armed Forces".

When I was younger, in my twenties, I was thinking I would be married. Now, as time passes, it becomes ever harder to make up my mind.

L.: I think you didn't find somebody to really get along with very well.

W.: O, maybe this as well, but you see, everybody in my family is divorced and it was not pleasant for any of them.

L.: Yes, you're right.

W.: From the emotional viewpoint, I am afraid of marriage because I am thinking of divorce. I have always lived in a family made up of women: mother, sister, grandmother and myself. There was nothing we thought that could not have been done by a woman. Mother was a very intelligent and capable woman and I grew up with respect and admiration for her. Nothing a man can do is impossible for me to do. I do sports and anything else, shooting, anything. (The transmission is discontinued for approximately 5 min.)

L.: In Yugoslavia, the Catholic Church is much more independent than here.

W.: Who comes immediately after CEAUȘESCU, What I mean to say is who would follow him in case...?

L.: There is a legal succession proceeding, there is the vice-president, the prime-minister, but it is very difficult to predict... it would be a long process.

W.: Isn't he preparing anybody to follow him?

L.: Not from the government, if he is really preparing somebody, that is his son, nevertheless...

W.: Are there family issues? (laughs)

L.: Immediately after him is ELENA, his wife, there is the Central Committee.

W.: A country governed by a family!

L.: Yes! There is an uncle who is in the government and many other relatives. This is the state system.

W.: It is weird and interesting! Many of us, who know little or too little about Romania, have a different image. CEAUŞESCU and Romania represent the "black sheep" in the communist system. All the criticisms CEAUŞESCU brings against the Russians and other things of this kind make an impression.

L.: CEAUŞESCU manages to get along by doing "somersaults" and other acrobatics, but the regime is as repressive and terrifying as the one in the U.S.S.R. Newspapers, for instance, from first to last page, only show his photographs. They recently returned from Cyprus, Malta and other places.... Cyprus was the last country visited, they met SPYROS KYPRIANOU. The photographs with him and ELENA fill pages.

W.: And don't people say anything?

L.: Not quite. The last who opened his mouth was PAUL GOMA, after that followed a disaster. But they are much more subtle (the government, the state) than the Russians. For instance, in the U.S.S.R., when you want to go someplace, you need to ask for permission. Not here, you may travel by car, by airplane, wherever you want. It is easier here.

W.: And journalists, can they openly tell the truth?

L.: By no means.

W.: But if they do it, what happens to them, are they going to prison?

L.: To prison? I am not aware, as far as I know, many Baptists, Protestants, are now in prison. Many Jews have been in jail, remnants of the former bourgeoisie. I think some of the inconvenient people are put into psychiatric hospitals.

W.: And how do people adjust to this environment?

L.: Differently or curiously according to their personalities. Some exhibit a sort of "sly innocence", but some are obviously opportunistic.

W.: But what is the difference between Romania and China?

L.: There is certainly a difference.

W.: There is, because Chinese are utterly cowardly. They have no money, they deliberately accept being robbed, they have no money, sometimes there is nothing to eat, but they have no choice. I met some Chinese in Las Vegas, they are so well-bred, so polite.

L.: This is a place where people compete with each other to become party members and get positions thanks to it. (W. laughs)

Don't laugh, I am serious. The ones who are party members and have positions are privileged. But whoever steps down from the top of the pyramid, nothing will stop him from falling all the way down.

W.: Nevertheless, the U.S.S.R. regime is totalitarian.

L.: There is no great difference. If you speak to the ones who come as members of delegations, to the U.S., you get the impression that there is a "Marxist paradise" there. But we, who live here, know what this paradise means. And there is not the slightest hope!

W.: Well, but it is rather developed from the industrial viewpoint.

L.: This is the worst part of all. *JIM MORGAN may have told you.*

W.: JIM MORGAN, ah, yes!

L.: From the economic viewpoint, it is here that communism stumbles.

W.: And is there no revolt foreseen!?

L.: No! If you would only see how CEAUŞESCU is greeted at the airport!

W.: How old are they?

L.: Rather old, they are 65-66. They celebrate their birthdays in January. A kind of national holiday. His wife is a scientist. Wrote a series of scientific books. The son is leader of the young communist organization. He has made a name for himself as a drunkard and lecher. He was elected president of the organization committee for the International Year of Youth.

And people have a very hard time. They queue for bread, butter, and meat.

W.: I also went out of the hotel in the morning and saw the queues. The most depressing sight. The masses of old people queuing! I have been to the G.D.R. and did not see such things.

L.: When have you been to the G.D.R.?

W.: In 1968.

L.: I was also in the G.D.R., in 1977. They have the highest living standard in Eastern Europe. They live very well.

Then they speak about a woman in Vienna, a mutual acquaintance, whose husband has died. They talk about BRUNO KREISKY, about his loss of popularity. (Dialogue ends.)

A.N.C.S.S.A., *Informative* fund, file no. 1093922, vol. IV, ff. 18-22.
Handwritten indication: "V./R.".
*Here and further down suspension points appear in the document.
**Handwritten indication in the document: "JESSIE HELMS – American senator, a member of the Republican Party".
***Here and further down underlined in the document.

-12-

Communication of the Bucharest Municipality Securitate to the 3rd Directorate within the Department of State Security, forwarding the note made by the informer "Dan" regarding the talks during a dinner offered in honor of Ernest Latham and James Morgan; "Dan" about Latham – "remarkable intellectual level"

Socialist Republic Romania*	Top Secret
Ministry of Internal Affairs	Copy no. 1
Department of State Security	
Securitate of Bucharest Municipality	
No. 122/C.T./D/00754445/198[3]	
File no.**	

To the 3rd Directorate / Serv. I

Find attached the copy of the briefing provided by our source "DAN", regarding the reception offered by the cultural attaché of the U.S. in Bucharest.

Deputy Chief Securitate of Bucharest Municipality

Colonel, SIG, RĂDUCĂ GHEORGHE

Chief of the Bureau, Major, SIG, MAIEREAN VASILE

C.T./N.C./2 copies/1 page/rd.00300/2080/11.15.1983

[Annex]

Top Secret

Copy no. 1

NOTE

On September 22 ***, 19.30, a dinner was offered by MERRY BLOCKER (adjunct cultural attaché U.S.A.) in honor of ERNEST LATHAM (cultural attaché) and JAMES MORGAN III (adjunct cultural attaché) and his wife. The dinner took place at M. BLOCKER's domicile, at str. M. Eminescu no. 123.

The general atmosphere was relaxed, emotional, vaguely confused. There was no formal introduction, as would have been customary, therefore, at a time very late in the evening (at the moment the dessert was being served), I personally requested to be shown who was the new cultural attaché. On the other hand, I was not introduced to J. MORGAN III or to his wife.

Most of the time I was engaged in conventional conversation with MERRY BLOCKER and ANCA GIURESCU, on the travels of the historian DINU GIURESCU and on history subjects. At a certain moment, there was a display of contradictory, opposing viewpoints, between A. GIURESCU and myself, on the baleful part played by England, and more precisely by British capitalism, of the Victorian sort, on European history****. While expressing such opinions unfavorable to England, I was confronted with a markedly philo-British attitude from ANCA GIURESCU, while M. BLOCKER tried to arbitrate with humor and common sense a dialogue which had become heated *****.

Another interlocutor was E. BRYAN SAMUEL, from the Economic Section of the U.S. Embassy, who sustained a lively discussion on literature and literary criticism, demonstrating a remarkable training in this field. Starting from this, I talked to him about the graduate studies by E.B. SAMUEL (at the University of Chicago) and about the system of American universities.

E.B. SAMUEL finally introduced me to E. LATHAM (the new cultural attaché), with whom I talked for a few minutes, at the end, in the presence of EDUARD McBRIDE and his wife. The talk proved to me that my interlocutor has a remarkable intellectual level. We initially talked about the syntheses of culture and literature offered to the Romanian reader by *Secolul XX* [magazine]. Among the subjects touched upon were issues of literary history pertaining to the penetration into the world circuit of the great English and American authors, emphasizing the importance of literary criticism and of the wide distribution of literary opinions in order to establish the great names, from WHITMAN to FAULKNER. My talk to E. LATHAM was stimulating, and my interlocutor declared to me at the end of the dialogue that he hoped we could speak again on this and other subjects.

At the dinner (which was not a sit down dinner, but a buffet), I also had the opportunity to meet the new director of the American Library in Bucharest, KIKI SKAGEN MUNSHI. The conversation with her was much more artificial, as K. MUNSHI talked about personal issues (such as the arrival of the cat she owns from Paris, by airplane)****** More special seemed to me her dialogue with a young Romanian specialist in the field of law and legislation, and I had the opportunity to learn a few interesting viewpoints on the Nigerian legislation and Constitution (a subject in which K. MUNSHI was rather competent). Nevertheless, speaking of her intellectual level, the interlocutor did not strike me as very brilliant, and the conversation (incidentally) made obvious some deficiencies of cultural information.

I have noticed among the guests ALEXA VISARION, RADU IONESCU, and others I did not know.

On Monday, September 26, C.Y., a reception took place at E. McBRIDE's residence, in honor of the same person. In an atmosphere dominated by a great congestion of guests, I had the opportunity to also meet J. MORGAN III and his wife, but only talked very briefly to them.

Due to the congestion, I stayed up almost to the end of the reception (18.30-20.00) talking to the Romania employees of the American Library, and I only took my leave from MERRY BLOCKER and MARY ANN IGNATIUS. Among other guests I noticed the RALIANs, the MONAFUs, the A.D. MUNTEANUs, A. PREDA, A. NICOLESCU, S. STOENESCU, R. MIHĂILĂ, from the English Chair, RADU IONESCU, ION HOBANA, ALEXA VISARION, ballerinas, painters, as well as a number of persons I had already seen at reception-dinners last week. There was in no way any special issue.

rd.00300/1966/3 copies/1 page/11.06.1983

A.N.C.S.S.A., Informative fund, file no. 1093922, vol. I, ff. 104-105.
Handwritten indication at the beginning of the document: "B.1/M.A.";
"11.16.1983".
* Emblem of the R.S.R.
** Rubric left blank.
*** Here and further down underlined in the document. Underlining followed by the handwritten indication: "Quite a while, if we think that we are only a few meters away from the S.B.M. and that the diplomat has meanwhile already left. / 11.17.1983 / Lt. Col., SIG, undecipherable".
**** Handwritten note: "There was no better place for such a dispute".
***** Handwritten note: "Poor her, what could she do??!!".
****** Handwritten note: "Who was to arrive by airplane: the cat or the owner?!".

-13-

Summary note by informer "Rodica" regarding the organization of the activity of the Press and Culture Section of the U.S. Embassy in Bucharest; Ernest Latham's profile and competencies - "employed by the C.I.A."; the diplomat does not miss any opportunity to point out that he holds the leading, decisive position; Latham: suspicious, self-important towards subordinates and representatives of Romanian institutions

311/M.A.   Top Secret

Inf. "RODICA"   Unique copy

File: 371/1972 / Register: 474   01.03.1984

House: "Continental"

NOTE

LATHAM's and MORGAN's arrival brought about a certain change in the manner of distributing tasks between EDWARDS and MERRY BLOCKER, after JACKOVICH's departure.

MORGAN is in charge of all issues concerning lecturers and grantees, both American and Romanian. LATHAM is in charge of exhibitions, American Participants in the cultural field, and any cultural event. In fact, he supervises, because he only adds conclusions to telegrams, while drawing up the answers, the letters, as well as the suggestions and initiatives revert to KIKI MUNSHI, MORGAN as well as some Romanian clerks*.

EDWARDS continues to be in charge of American Participants in the other fields.

Up to now, the Library had its independent activity, although it was coordinated by the cultural attaché, a thing introduced once JACKO-VICH arrived. One of the measures taken by LATHAM was to involve the Library and respectively KIKI MUNSHI in active participation in the case of all persons he is in charge of. As he is highly hesitant and obviously his knowledge is sometimes doubtful even in the area of American culture, he is counting on KIKI MUNSHI, on MORGAN, sometimes even on EDWARDS and, to the same extent, on some Romanian diplomats in order to carry out all the works related to different phases in order to modernize various programs. The subordination relationship of KIKI MUNSHI and MORGAN versus LATHAM is obvious, the latter never missing any opportunity to stress, through his attitude and behavior, that the leadership and decision-making are his.

In general, I do not have the impression that he devotes too much of his time to activities related to the issues he is in charge of. After 11-12.00, he has Romanian language lessons at the Library or leaves for the central building of the Embassy and only returns in the afternoon, around 4.00.

He is extremely self-important, not only towards his subordinates, but also towards the representatives of different Romanian institutions. He is trenchant and always wants to have the last word. Probably it was imposed on him and he imposed on himself to adopt a hard line, on the one side, in order to demonstrate how intransigent he is and, maybe, in order to hide his lack of firmness and of certain knowledge.

Up to now, KIKI MUNSHI has always shown herself to be very willing to be cooperative and to help him in all circumstances, proving to be creative and full of benevolence, while MORGAN, even if he very conscientiously fulfills all tasks imposed by LATHAM, he is obviously lacking any enthusiasm and sometimes gives the impression he is despising him.

As LATHAM befriended the ambassador from the very beginning, a certain distance was created between him and the other diplomats in the Cultural Section, McBRIDE included, with the exception of EDWARDS, of course.

It is very difficult to work with him, as he is very much lacking malleability. He acts in a linear manner and sometimes is obtuse. In addition, he is extremely suspicious and any assertions or issues raised are bound to arouse his doubts, that he has the impression either that something is dissimulated, or that there is an intention to mislead him.

He is very interested in buying books and objects, for which he spends considerable amounts, in contrast with his constant manner of manifestation in different circumstances. He is interested in all sorts of books, especially history, especially those referring to the history of the Dacians and the Romans.

He very assiduously studies Romanian language, leaving the impression that he understands it perfectly, but obviously avoids speaking it. He speaks German rather well and manifests a disguised interest for the culture and history of the Saxons in Transylvania.

I heard that during a conversation he said he was an officer in the reserves.

Note

Approximately two months after the arrival of the diplomat, I asked the informer to prepare a summary on his activity. As also results from information received by us in other ways, "LASCU" is employed by the American Information Service. In this respect, it is significant to take into consideration his relation to "EMIL" and the ambassador and the attitude of contempt shown by McBRIDE versus the two of them.

Although he cannot stand him, JIM MORGAN executes "LASCU"'s orders. I propose to make together with the collective chief an analysis of the case at the Bureau chief, in order to initiate proceedings of surveillance of "LASCU"'s activity.

Lt. Col., SIG, undecipherable

A.N.C.S.S.A., *Informative* fund, file no. 1093922, vol. I, ff. 118-120.
Handwritten indication at the beginning of document: "V./LASCU".
*Underlined here and in the rest of the document.

-14-

Note by informer "Cezar" regarding the audience of lecturer Thomas Carlson, accompanied by Ernest Latham, at the Ministry of Education; the Ministry – discontent with the lecturer's writings, Latham – "he has the right to write what he wants and to publish what he wishes, this is a proof of American democracy"

311/M.A.	Top Secret
Source "CEZAR"	Unique copy
File* / Register**	03.16.1984

NOTE

On 03.16.1984, the American lecturer from the University of Bucharest, THOMAS CARLSON, was invited for a discussion at the Ministry of Education. He published in the United States some articles including derogatory aspects about our country. To the surprise of the Ministry of Education team, the American diplomats "LASCU", cultural attaché, and "MARCU", deputy cultural attaché, also showed up at the meeting.

After the representatives of the Ministry expressed their dissatisfaction that the American lecturer wrote the mentioned articles, the diplomat "LASCU" took the floor and said that lecturer CARLSON was an American citizen and the Constitution of the United States gave him the right to write what he wanted and to publish what he wished, this being a proof of American democracy.

Then the representatives of the Ministry told him that the American lecturer should have watched with objectivity the developments in our society and report them objectively, not tendentiously, playing in the game of whoever had him write the texts.

"LASCU" indignantly advocated that nobody had him write the articles and that the lecturer did it on his own initiative.

Then "LASCU" insolently asked: "What may happen if CARLSON will continue to write articles about Romania?"

The appropriate officials answered that it was not desirable that the lecturer should continue to write untruths or express personal views regarding the political and social life in our country. The diplomat "LASCU" ironically enquired: "But what will happen if Mr. CARLSON no longer writes about your country?"

The source was certain that "LASCU" intended to turn this issue into a sort of blackmail in order to obtain promises from the Ministry along the line of improving the cultural exchange relations between ourselves and the Americans. He was answered that Mr. CARLSON may continue to write, but in an objective manner, not urged on by some specific person.

Then, seeing that the Romanian responded without fear, "LASCU" said that the Embassy was not to blame in connection with this issue and again invoked the provisions of the American Constitution, which give CARLSON the right to write whatever he wants.

The Embassy was an official body and cannot interfere in such issues, meaning to say he could not prevent CARLSON from writing. Then he was told that, as a matter of fact, the Ministry had only invited CARLSON and it was a surprise that he was accompanied by the two diplomats. "LASCU" accepted the affront and asked that the floor should be given to CARLSON.

To everybody's surprise, CARLSON adopted a correct attitude, namely he said he was sorry for what had happened and had he known that the subjects mentioned in his articles would annoy the Romanians, he would not have written them. He even wanted to know which fragments were considered offensive.

Then he affirmed he very much regretted, the more so as he felt very comfortable in our country and people were extremely warm and friendly and he was provided optimum conditions to teach classes, he made friends with people that deserve his entire respect and he was considering asking to stay one more year.

At that moment, the diplomat "LASCU" regarded him surprised at first and then with contempt, probably because CARLSON had completely strayed from the briefing made by the diplomat.

The Ministry team told him they would analyze extending his stay for one more year, but, as a rule, approvals are not granted for a third year, and therefore it is possible that his request will be rejected.

It is worth mentioning that the diplomat "MARCU" never said a word during those forty-five minutes; on the other hand he wrote down everything that was said almost word for word, to a total of approximately seven pages.

Upon leaving, the Ministry team told the diplomats that for the 1984-1985 academic year, all American grantees had been accepted, with the exception of EATON, who had requested to return to Iaşi. Without any further comment, the Americans said they will convey this fact to Washington.

There were no other issues.

N.O.

These happenings also show that the American lecturers and PhD candidates are maneuvered by the diplomats in the Cultural Section of the Embassy in order to fulfill the tasks they should fulfill, especially along the line of ideological influencing and diversion. These aspects are clearly apparent from CARLSON's declaration and "LASCU"'s attitude.

Lt. Col., SIG, undecipherable

A.N.C.S.S.A., *Informative* fund, file no. 1093922, vol. I, ff. 159-160.
Handwritten indication at the beginning of the document: 1) "LASCU";
2) "Exploited / R.".
* Rubric left blank.
** Rubric left blank.

-15-

Rendition of the recording of the conversation among Ernest Latham, Morgan, Melanie Munshi and Dean Kramer; Munshi "the living conditions are difficult, everything is exported, and especially food"; Latham: "the Soviets accuse the Romanians of nationalism and goad the Hungarians against them"

03.21.1984

SPECIAL OPERATION
DINNER AT THE RESTAURANT "DOI COCOȘI"

1) LATHAM

2) MORGAN

3) KIKI MUNSHI

4) DEAN KRAMER, pianist

After a short historical presentation about Romania, with an emphasis on the moment of the "Union" and its impact on the Hungarian minority – he stressed the fact that the Hungarians were dispersed to other areas of the country, and Romanians were moved into their place. The head of the Catholic Church is in Alba Iulia. All these explanations are provided by LATHAM.

KIKI M. says the population has a very hard time, the living conditions are difficult, everything is exported, and especially food, in order to get hard currency. People suffer, they cannot leave the country, and they lack freedom of speech.

LATHAM says that all key positions in the state are held by N. CEAUȘESCU and his family (wife, brother, son). Also tells him that N.C.'s reputation on the international level is owed to his nonconformity versus the Soviets. The Soviets accuse Romanians of nationalism and goad the Hungarians against them.

(LATHAM and the American guest have this conversation separately, while the others discuss unimportant matters.)*

They discuss the social system from a philosophical viewpoint, the role of the individual and the conflict between the system and the individual. The guest makes an analysis of circumstances in Poland, which generated a government and systemic crisis.

LATHAM tells him that much of the press and mass media in general, distort reality and present it in an untrue manner, which, in his opinion, is not the case to the same extent in the G.D.R., where press is somewhat more objective. (From his observations, it is clear that the guest is extremely clever, with a solid knowledge of sociology, political science, philosophy, and economics).

Then they pass on to more "innocent" subjects: circus as an art, the history of the Soviet circus.

They discuss about "Safari"; exotic animals, etc.

They talk about sports – "jogging", which is fashionable, and LATHAM recounts that in a magazine of the Department of State there was an article about an American employed by the U.S. Embassy in Congo, who was shot while jogging and the decision was taken to wear little flags (miniatures of the American flag), in order for them not to be attacked in error. The person was mistaken for a Soviet diplomat.

LATHAM says PERRY DAY was at the post in [Germany]** when the hostages in Iran were freed and he was in charge of bringing them to America. (Up to the end – nothing of interest).

A.N.C.S.S.A., *Informative* fund, file no. 1093922, vol. IV, p. 82.
*Here and further down in the document round parentheses of the officer who rendered the recording.
**Parenthesis of the editor.

-16-

Report by D.S.S., based on the account of in-former "Alina", regarding her warning on Ernest Latham - "an extremely dangerous person, not only for the Romanians, also for the Americans"

311/H.C.   Top Secret

"ALINA"   Unique copy

                                       07.12.1984

REPORT

"ALINA" was warned by FRANK URSINO regarding ERNEST LATHAM, cultural attaché, whom URSINO had known for a long time, since LATHAM was working in Berlin. He characterized him as an extremely dangerous person, not only for the Romanians, also for the Americans, and especially regarding women. This because after the matrimonial failure he had suffered, LATHAM has a powerful resentment against women in general.

N.B.

ERNEST LATHAM has the attention of ind. 311/M.A., where this note will be exploited.

Lt.-maj., SIG, undecipherable

A.N.C.S.S.A., *Informative* fund, file no. 1093922, vol. I, p. 232.

-17-

Summary by informer "Ionescu" regarding his meetings with the diplomat Ernest Latham in March-July 1984; Latham: "perfectly fit for fostering relationships, nonintrusive, extremely vast erudition"

S.M.B./544/A.N.

Source: "IONESCU"

Date: 07.23.1984

SUMMARY ON THE SERIES OF MEETINGS WITH MR. ERNEST HARGREAVES LATHAM JR., FIRST SECRETARY AND CULTURAL ATTACHÉ OF THE U.S. EMBASSY IN BUCHAREST

First meeting:

At a dinner offered in March 1984 by the British ambassador, Mr. PHILIP McKEARNEY, at his residence, ERNEST LATHAM was introduced to me by Mrs. McKEARNEY.

Series of subsequent meetings (initiated by the fact that I was contacted, by phone, by employees of the American Embassy using my calling card):

– "Capşa", my initiative: outstanding consideration concerning Romanian culture, concerning my personal achievements. He delivered to me a scientific correspondence from the U.S., which had been in his possession for a long time (nothing significant, a pretext).

– "Capşa", his initiative: same note.

– His domicile: meeting together with SAMUEL BUGAN, intense conversations, scholarly atmosphere.

– "Bulevard", my invitation: we resumed friendly meetings after his travelling abroad.

– His domicile, together with my wife and KIKI MUNSHI, director of the American Library: scholarly meeting, but with more of a friendly note.

– My home: a general, morning meeting: propositions for a study trip to be made by me in the U.S.A.

– "Bulevard", then his domicile: meeting started with DIANA BELINSKAYA, then with him alone. Mainly dedicated to how to assure me a study trip to the U.S.A.

– "Manuc", my invitation: continuation of the previous talk.

– "Manuc", his invitation: conclusions of previous talks and adopting future procedures.

(Meanwhile, we spoke several times over the phone.)

Character of the partner in dialogue:

– culture, manners, style, diplomacy: impeccable, perfectly fit for fostering relationships, nonintrusive, extremely vast erudition, always very attentive regarding the cultural level of the talks.

– attitude versus Romania: judging from all present evidence, very positive. It is important that he has a multilateral knowledge of our culture and history.

– personal relationships: seems to show the positive side of the American nature, the wish to be involved in helping the others, quite largely open. Extensive caution (does not mention other Romanian names, does not want to enter subjects that are not in his competence or that have a wide philosophical character).

– politics: he does not seem uninfluenced by a propaganda unfavorable to Romanians, but is less influenced than most of the Westerners.

He is responsive to profound arguments, and not to superficial matters. He is extremely cautious in this respect.

Prediction with respect to him:

– he may prove useful in personal relations (remains to be seen whether on a small, moderate, or large scale).

– may be assisted to learn even more profoundly Romanian culture, from the angle of friendly reactions.

– he will most likely act in a favorable way for Romania. If he does not do it, that would mean either that he has strict orders in that regard, or that a mistake was made, regardless by whom, in the relationships with him.

Reasons for this relationship (from his viewpoint) could only be inferred, the ones below are merely my assumptions:

– Reports and characterizations made by foreigners I have met here, in the U.S. or in other parts. I know for sure such reports are made. They may be discussed among the different sections at the Embassy. These reports are sketches, arguments, and lifework (Prof. WILLIAM ULHICK observed to me: "It is understood (or known) that you are one of the most important personalities of science, etc."). Nevertheless ERNEST LATHAM displayed directly only a very slight interest in the scientific side of my scientific activity.

– It is easy to observe that both my way of approaching science, and of writing are more readily assimilated and better correspond to the Western way of working and expressing. (I have done and educated myself in this manner precisely in order to be able to communicate our cultural results.)

– There is an interest in the Western World for persons who are at any time capable to make more intelligible aspects of cultures and societies in Eastern Europe, as well as other subjects more difficult to assimilate by the Atlantic countries.

– I have tried to discuss as profoundly as possible, using my English, which is far from perfect, in a manner as simple as can be, the topical subjects, expressing realities and avoiding the conventional blabber.

Problems referring to myself that have been discussed:

– From the first meeting, he wanted to deal with the literary work published by me, in the sense of translating, of our correlation, of finding ways to publish it. We have made some beginnings in this respect. For the moment, I gave priority to other aspects.

– Subsequently (meetings three-four), I in my turn asked for support in order to publish there philosophical-psychological writings, in essay style. I was made certain promises, some translation samples will have to be made.

– During the meetings at my home, ERNEST LATHAM suggested I should make a longer study visit in the U.S.A. (three-four months up to a year).

– I have contacted DIANA BELINSKAYA for preparations in view of my travel project.

– He explored the possibility that my stay in the U.S. should extend to two years and for me to be involved in teaching (sessions or courses) at highly prestigious institutions in Boston (M.I.T.), Chicago (Univ.) or Philadelphia (Univ.).

– He asked for my autobiography and a work schedule, in order to obtain the necessary support for financing the project; this is the latest stage reached during our discussions.

N.O.

Note will be exploited, as a copy, at the 3rd Dir.

SIG, undecipherable

A.N.C.S.S.A., *Informative* fund, file no. 1093922, vol. I, ff. 269-275.
Handwritten indication: "The material was received on 04.18.1986".

-18-

Communication by the 3rd Directorate within D.S.S. to the Military Base 0610/Bucharest, regarding the acceptance for doctoral studies of the diplomats Ernest Latham and Melanie Mun-shi

Ministry of Internal Affairs	Top Secret
Department of State Security	S.P. 395
MB 0625	Copy no.*
No. M.A./D/00170816/9 August, 1984	

To MB 0610 – Bucharest

In answer to your communication D/001615/213 of 08.03.1984, be informed that we agree to accept for post-graduate studies against payment in hard currency for the academic year 1984-1985 of the American diplomats ERNEST LATHAM, cultural attaché, and KIKI SKAGEN MUNSHI, director of the American Library in Bucharest.

Commander of the Base, Major General, ALEXIE ȘTEFAN

A.N.C.S.S.A., *Informative* fund, file no. 1093922, vol. I, p. 240.
*Rubric left blank.

-19-

Note by MB 0672/Bucharest, to the 3ʳᵈ Directorate within D.S.S., regarding movement of
diplomats Ernest Latham and William Edwards in
Bucharest, on 13 August, 1984

Ministry of Internal Affairs   Top Secret

Department of State Security   Unique copy

MB 0672 Bucharest

No. D/00478039 of 08.18.1984

To MB 0625/311
NOTE

On 08.13.1984, at *10.15** "LASCU" and "EMIL" walked from the U.S. Consulate along Snagov Street, then Batistei, crossed N. Bălcescu Blvd., stopped in front of the windows of the "Elegant" shop, looked at the displayed shoes, then continued along 13 Decembrie Street, *Calea Victoriei, entered the Kretzulescu Passage and, under the pretext of looking at the church, "EMIL" drew "LASCU"'s attention to the parking lot, at the many cars (approximately 8) having the same brand of aerials, then discreetly pointed out to him the entrance between the handicraft and the book shop (headquarters of the M.I.).*

Then they entered the "Antiquary Bookstore", where they leafed through several books in various fields, "EMIL" consulted the "History of the Bible", and "LASCU" bought two magazines of natural sciences. Afterwards, they came out and entered the new book shop.

In the book shop, they looked at the displayed books, some of which they leafed for approximately 10′, then left along Calea Victoriei, the Palace Square, entered the shop *"Stirex", looking at* the displayed merchandise, then left along C.A. Rosetti Street, crossed N. Bălcescu Blvd., and then went along it and entered the tie shop "Adonis", close to the Italian Church.

After 1, "EMIL" came out of the shop, looked at its windows and at the persons coming from the direction they had also come from, and when "LASCU" also came out, they went on together along N. Bălcescu Blvd., Batistei Street, "EMIL" greeted from outside the lady working at the "Air Algerie" company, who was at her desk, then they both went to the Consulate, entering there at 11.10.

Note: During the entire trip, "EMIL" gave priority to "LASCU", showing him attention and respect.

We attach 5 (five) photographs and the negatives.

Deputy Commander of Base, SIG, undecipherable**

Chief of Bureau, Lt. Col., SIG, undecipherable

A.N.C.S.S.A., *Informative* fund, file no. 1093922, vol. I, ff. 245-246.
Handwritten indication at the beginning of the document: "M.A./Serv.14".
*Here and further down underlined in the document.
**The seal of the respective military base was applied.

-20-

Notes by informer "Ionescu" regarding his visit to the residence of diplomat Ernest Latham; "Ionescu" - "our genuine meeting with the West can be built upon cultural pillars"; again him - "It is the moment to conquer by means of an active Romanian ideology, of the sort of Lucian Blaga's"

MJR ALDEA NIC.

SOURCE: "IONESCU"

S.M.B./No. 0544   Oct. 1984

[NOTE]
MEETING WITH PERSONS FROM THE U.S. EMBASSY

Wednesday, October 10, 1984, I was invited to Mr. ERNEST LAT-HAM's home. Mrs. MUNSHI was also present. This meeting, as well as the following, addressed a specific subject. We were to discuss the program of my eventual grant in the U.S.A.

We met in front of "Eminescu" book store, at 13.00. Mr. LATHAM came by car, together with Mrs. MUNSHI. We all went to his place. We had established to meet in the circumstances already known – I am not coming back to them. Everything started very well. I was shown much courtesy. The dinner had also more splendor than usual. I offered little gifts (two engravings to the host and some home-made plum brandy to Mrs. MUNSHI). Mrs. MUNSHI fetched the materials we were to talk about. They were placed ready at hand. The talk was extremely lively, on cultural issues, vaguely touching politics. Nothing relevant or engaging. The pressure of the dialogue was operated by Mrs. MUNSHI with a special technique (debate, criticizing both East and West, everything, but nothing in a specific way). Several hours went by and then she suddenly announced she was leaving. Given the purpose of the meeting, which had been totally neglected*, I also said that I was leaving. We were both given a lift by Mr. LATHAM. Mrs. MUNSHI took along the materials about which we were to discuss, without saying a word.

Under the circumstances, I reacted relatively brusquely, saying I did not see when we could have a more concrete conversation. The two of them seemed surprised and, in front of the American Library, started pondering on their schedule to establish a new meeting. In order not to [receive] excuses and hear subterfuges, I said they may consider themselves invited to my place any time. Thursday, October 18 was settled on. Mrs. MUNSHI stepped down at the Library, I was brought up to Palace Square.

Nevertheless, I was displeased with the manner in which the meeting had unfurled – I had the sensation that my reactions were put to the test. Only one hour after we had parted, I phoned Mr. LATHAM at his home and told him that I wanted to see him once more before Thursday. He seemed touched. We decided to shortly meet on Friday, October 12, 11.00, at the brasserie "Capşa". I intended to show my slight dissatisfaction during the meeting. That was not the case, because he took over the dialogue, promising a rapid settlement of my grant in the U.S.A. When he opened this subject, I had made no mention of my reason for asking to meet him. The rest of the discussion had a general character. Nevertheless, they need an explanation. I will make it, further down. We took our leave one hour later, upon my request, as I had a meeting at the Institute.

The meeting on Thursday, 18, had to be postponed under the known circumstances. I have conveyed, over the phone, through two female interlocutors, in two brief conversations, as I did not reach him in person, an invitation for Thursday, October 25. When I could speak to him on Friday, at the Embassy, he said that day was not suitable, but accepted that the meeting should take place at my place, on Monday, Oct. 29, 16.00. Realizing it may have displeased him by not attending the exhibition of American theatre, I called him once again and told him I wanted to go there on Tuesday, Oct. 23, a day when he himself was going to be out of Bucharest. He asked me to phone Mrs. MUNSHI next Tuesday for her to secure me the tickets.

During the talk, Mrs. MUNSHI told me how to find the reserved tickets, but also that the meeting on Monday, 29, cannot take place, as there is an official banquet. There was also a trip to Germany (I did not understand who was to travel), therefore Mr. LATHAM asked me to call him up on Wednesday (at the Embassy, in the afternoon, possibly at home). This request for an urgent call makes me think he may suggest a quick meeting. We shall see.

A concrete aspect of the talks: the issue of medical books previously mentioned. I saw them at Mr. LATHAM's home. They are not at all objectionable – at least judging from the general titles (they are actually not books, but magazines), but they lack an outstanding scientific significance. He would want me to look them over.

The most important general aspect: the overall nuance of talks about Romania is favorable, but not resolute enough. During my travels to both Europe and the U.S., I came to the firm belief that everyone in the West looks forward to transforming the American-Soviet opposition into an opposition between Russia's neighbors and Russia itself. And this conflict may be successful as several Poland-type situations emerge. This is why the Western propaganda favors in turn these countries, favors economically one or the other among the Eastern friends, etc. I could explain this in detail. In Germany and France, this attitude is cultivated at the widest level. To my belief, the U.S. are cleaner from the viewpoint of the population's opinion. I hope that a proper cultural action in America would create an attitude favorable to us. Our genuine meeting with the West can be built upon cultural pillars. It is along these lines that I have tried to [conduct] my discussions.

One may proceed even more actively, as I have shown. It is the moment to conquer by means of an active Romanian ideology, of the sort of LUCIAN BLAGA**.

A.N.C.S.S.A., *Informative* fund, file no. 1093922, vol. I, ff. 276-283.
Handwritten indication at the beginning of the note: "The material was received on 03.18.1986".
*Here and further down underlined in the document.
**Handwritten indication at the end of the note: "Subsequent meetings. / Where?"

-21-

Action plan of the 3rd Directorate within D.S.S. in the Information Surveillance Dossier regarding the cultural attaché Ernest Latham; operative and information proceedings in order to "document and unmask the espionage activity carried out by the diplomat"; he "conducts his espionage activity by visiting bookshops and especially antique stores"

311/M.A.   Top Secret

Unique copy

11.08.1984

I approve,

Lt. Col., SIG, undecipherable

ACTION PLAN IN I.S.D. "LASCU" CONCERNING THE AMERICAN DIPLOMAT LATHAM ERNEST HARGREAVES

The American diplomat LATHAM ERNEST HARGREAVES occupied his position as cultural attaché in September 1983.

He was born on 08.11.1938 in Massachusetts – U.S.A. He graduated Dartmouth College – U.S.A. in 1960, then joined the U.S. Army as a lieutenant. In 1966, he got a doctorate at Roosevelt University, then, in August, the same year, he was employed by the U.S.I.A. as an intern. After a training stage in Arabic language, he was appointed a deputy attaché in Berlin, within the Cultural Section.

From 1970 to 1973 he operated in Vienna as a deputy press and culture attaché, then he was called back to Washington, where he attended a course of Greek language. In 1974, he was appointed cultural attaché in Nicosia, whence he was called back to headquarters in 1977. In 1978 he was sent to work within the American Military Mission in West Berlin. Before coming to take over his position at the U.S Embassy in Bucharest, the diplomat attended a course of Romanian language in Washington.

As a result of surveillance carried out lately on the diplomat "LASCU", as well as on the occasion of analyses performed by the chief of the bureau and the chief of the group the conclusion was reached that he is enrolled in the C.I.A.*, assigned to collect information in the social-political and cultural areas.

In order to prevent an information leak as well as to document and unmask the espionage activities carried out by the diplomat against our country, the following informative-operative measures are to be taken:

1) "LASCU", alongside diplomat "EMIL", with whom he is in very close relations, was witnessed on several occasions to be concerned with knowing and supervising premises of the M.I., resorting as a cover to various subterfuges and efforts to conceal their activities.

In order to document their activities, fixed points of observation will be periodically set up near the premises targeted by the diplomats "LASCU" and "EMIL". As the suspicion exists that they may be carrying transmitter and receiving equipment in order to record codified messages, this aspect will also be prioritized at the time of observations.

Deadline: permanent

In charge: Lt. Col. MILITARU A.

2) Recently, the diplomats "LASCU" and "EMIL" have been seen entering a block of flats on one of the main city roads, after the diplomat "EMIL" undertook proceedings of self-surveillance and of assurance in view of diplomat "LASCU"'s safely entering the building. When entering the building, the diplomat "LASCU" was carrying an object he was

carefully concealing. The analysis of the case shows, in first instance, that the equipment used by "LASCU" may be a portable apparatus to listen to phone conversations of persons of interest to the two diplomats.

In order to determine the diplomats' activities, proceedings to control operative moments will be carried out, using the necessary equipment to this end.

Deadline: permanent

In charge: Lt. Col. MILITARU A.

3) According to the reports of the operative authority, as well as other information sources, the conclusion was drawn that the diplomat "LASCU" is using in his espionage activity the method of visiting bookstores and especially antique book stores, a method used by some of his predecessors as well.

Recently, "LASCU" visited, in circumstances that are extremely suspicious, the antique bookstore on Calea Moşilor, and remained alone in a room of the store for over half an hour, while being secured at the entrance by the diplomat "MELANIA", who reportedly behaved in a suspicious manner and showed signs of restlessness all the while. It results from the analysis of data that "LASCU" is making use of antique bookstores in connection with his system for getting information.

In order to document his activity and to identify the traitors in the ranks of Romanian citizens, strict measures of intelligence surveillance of the diplomat's activities will be taken, as well as of the Romanian citizens who visit the book store shortly after the diplomat has left and behave in a suspicious manner.

The respective store saleswoman will be checked on and kept under watch.

Deadline for surveillance: permanent

Deadline for checkup and surveillance

of the saleswoman: 01.12.1984

In charge: Lt. Col. MILITARU ALEX.

4) Intelligence sources have reported that the diplomat "LASCU" is meeting at his residence on Str. Plantelor 37 with the student of color "NORA". She is a student in medicine and lives in a block with many foreign students. Her husband, an American citizen and a petroleum engineer by profession, used to work for two years as a specialist in our country. During that time, he kept a permanent connection with C.I.A. staff in the U.S. Embassy in Bucharest. "NORA's" intelligence surveillance has shown that she is linked to Romanian citizens who hold secrets or intend to emigrate.

Measures will be taken in order to find out "NORA's" activity and her preoccupations along the line of information gathering, as well as Romanian citizens she is connected with. At the same time, measures will be taken to control contacts between the diplomat and the student "NORA".

Deadline: permanent

In charge: Lt. Col. MILITARU ALEX.

5) Lately, the diplomat has been associated with the Romanian citizen "CAROL", a specialist and holder of secrets, who works in an important institution in the capital. The conclusion drawn from these contacts, controlled by security means, is that the diplomat is carrying out an operation of knowing and studying the Romanian specialist, for the purpose of recruiting him. "CAROL", who is under surveillance, has met, under suspicious circumstances, with the diplomat "MELANIA" somewhere in the province, while "MELANIA" is working under "LASCU's" permanent guidance.

For the purpose of exposing the diplomat's and "CAROL's activities, measures of permanent control of his contacts will be taken, using security means.

Deadline: permanent

In charge: Lt. Col. MILITARU ALEX.

6) "LASCU" is in charge of the visits to our country of American specialists who hold conferences at the American Library and at various institutions in the capital and provinces. On the occasion of such visits, the American specialists establish contacts with some Romanian specialists, contacts that are maintained through "LASCU". The diplomat is further in charge with assigning grants to Romanian specialists who are the focus of attention of American espionage. Steps will be taken in order to learn about the diplomat's relationships and the mechanism due to which they have visited our country.

Deadline: permanent

In charge: Lt. Col. MILITARU ALEX.

7) Finding out and selecting for the purpose of recruiting and steering into the diplomat's area Romanian diplomats who have been posted to countries where "LASCU" has worked previous to his arrival in Bucharest, as well as of Romanian specialists, Ph.D. candidates or cooperative individuals who have worked in the respective countries and who may be of interest for the diplomat.

Deadline: 12.01.1984

In charge: Lt. Col. MILITARU ALEX.

In January 1985, the operation will be re-analyzed by the chief of the bureau and, according to the information which will emerge and the results of the pursuit surveillance of the diplomat, the action plan will be supplemented with new tasks, aimed at preventing the leak of information to the American diplomat, as well as documenting and revealing the espionage activity carried out by him on the territory of our father-land.

Officer specialist III, Lt. Col. MILITARU ALEX.

A.N.C.S.S.A., *Informative* fund, file no. 1093922, vol. I, ff. 4-6.
*Underlined here and in the rest of the document.

-22-

Note by informer "Ionescu" regarding his meet-ings with Ernest Latham on February 20 and March 6, 1985; Latham – "a man who has out-standing knowledge of Romanian history and cul-ture, at the same time a man of benevolence"

Ministry of Internal Affairs	Top Secret
Bucharest Municipality Securitate	Unique copy
Source "IONESCU"	March 1985

[NOTE]
MEETINGS WITH MR. ERNEST HARGREAVES LATHAM
ON FEBRUARY 20 AND MARCH 6, 1985

Although they bring up some of the most important points, these meeting have been among the least exciting, lacking any outstanding subjects.

The meeting on Feb. 20 was planned, at ERNEST LATHAM's in-sistence, approximately one month before. We settled certain details by phone. The host had announced his intention to invite the priest of the Anglican Church as well, the reason being his interest in philosophy (he is completing a Ph.D. in Switzerland on a theological subject with many philosophical implications, as it was explained to me).

It was a supper from 7.00 to approx. 10.30 p.m.

Upon my arrival at ERNEST LATHAM's, there was another guest, about whose presence I had not been aware. I did not catch her name when she introduced herself, and I did not make an effort to learn it. I understood she was working in American diplomacy, in Bonn, and she had come on a mission to the Embassy in Bucharest for a four month period. She was to return to Germany the following day. Reverend Mr. JOHN KEEFER came late. At the end of the dinner, I was the first to leave.

From the very beginning of the conversation, ERNEST LATHAM came back to the idea of my future travel to the U.S.A. He made it spontaneously and in a manner that seemed to me absolutely original. He was much more straightforward, saying he was convinced he would satisfy the main issue regarding this invitation.

Referring to the first talk on this issue, initiated by him (I realized he perfectly remembered it)*, he said that, as he had then anticipated, I only have to cross our frontier and I would find then the opportunity to study. He advanced again his opinion, very favorably commenting on my intellectual qualifications. Upon declining my thanks, he did not advance anything inappropriate or suggest anything in particular. It was perhaps the shortest conversation with him on this matter, but the impression it left on me was more serious than before.

Immediately afterwards the conversations were carried on in a very relaxed mood, almost indifferent considering the persons present, very calm and general. I did not feel under scrutiny – as I had felt on other occasions. The person from Bonn seemed a very common interlocutor. The Reverend, Mr. KEEFER, referred mainly to complementary matters, such as Orthodox, Catholic and Anglican customs. He discussed religious problems, especially from an historical and literary angle, almost detached and less directly than the rest of us, the other three persons present.

The style of the meeting seemed to conceal something different, a change.

Nevertheless, ERNEST LATHAM did not let me understand that he is to leave imminently for the F.R.G. I understood this for the first time, at a reception offered by the British cultural attaché**, Mr. KEVIN McGRINCESS, in conversation with Mr. EDWARD McBRIDE, who was also present at the event.

Within the context of our discussions, and taking into consideration the more private character of the meeting, I invited ERNEST LATHAM, together with JOHN KEEFER at a lunch, at the Chinese restaurant, on March 6, 12.30. At the same time, I separately invited Mr. McBRIDE, for a lunch on Wednesday, March 13, 12.30, at "Bucharest" restaurant. The invitations were accepted.

During the meeting at the Chinese restaurant, the atmosphere changed when compared to the one on February 20. We stayed at the table long after lunch itself was over. I brought ERNEST LATHAM an older Romanian book and an essay of mine – which is to be published in Steaua – on the ballad "Miorița", in which he is very much interested. In his turn, he had prepared for me a bottle of cognac as a gift. The two guests discussed with each other, as if it had been a self-evident matter, certain day-by-day details regarding my future presence in the U.S.A., as, for example, living conditions (they were probably referring to the North Carolina Univ.). I did not insist on more details. As for the rest, there was absolutely no private aspect, tensions, etc.

There are two issues which seem to me of primary importance in all this new experience:

– As I am so far away from all aspects of diplomatic gossip, peddling of rumors or information, which have nothing to do with my professional work or creation, I could all the time remain sincerely detached from issues such as LATHAM's travel to Germany or any other such matters. Probably they thus did not make me witness inappropriate behavior regarding my own invitation to the U.S.A. I hope things will remain this way.

– ERNEST LATHAM is a person deserving all the attention as a man who has outstanding knowledge of Romanian history and culture, at the same time a man of benevolence – to the extent I am able to judge these things. I am referring to the fact that, on March 6, he made for KEEFER a historical presentation of the 1918 Union, as well as on the condition of Romanians who today are outside the borders of Romania, a presentation such as I myself would not have been able to make, as I am simultaneously preoccupied and not aware of the current state of affairs.

I am also noting that a change in the situation is still at any time possible and deduce, correctly, I believe, E. McBRIDE's importance.

A.N.C.S.S.A., Informative fund, file no. 1093922, vol. I, ff. 338-343.
Handwritten indication: "The material was received on 03.18.1986".
*Underlined here and in the rest of the document.
**Underlining in document accompanied by exclamation mark.

-23-

Summary by informer "Ionescu" regarding the personality of diplomat Ernest Latham. He is serious in his intellectual preoccupations, favorable to Romania and Romanian culture. "If there were no functional and national barriers, he would probably be an ideal friend"

S.M.B./544/ALDEA NIC.   [Top Secret]

Source "IONESCU"   [March 1985]

NOTE

Mr. ERNEST HARGREAVES LATHAM JR.*, cultural attaché of the U.S.A. Embassy in Bucharest, is a profoundly cultivated person, extremely serious in his intellectual preoccupations, eager to behave devotedly with regard to the people close to him.

General framework of personality: exactly like his hierarchical superior, Mr. McBRIDE, he seems deeply dedicated to the interests of his country, capable of following closely in conduct the expectations of his institution. His intellectual profundity and volume of knowledge are amazing. He is able to make himself extremely attractive thanks to the interest he demonstrates regarding the people close to him or mere acquaintances, demonstrating his concern and care for them. He seems to have been working in truly problematic places in the world and to have secured for himself a sound professional status.

Temperament: He is warm and forthcoming. If it weren't for the functional and national barriers, he would probably be an ideal friend. He has a kind disposition and never becomes unpleasant. Perhaps one senses in him the responsibility of raising his little daughter alone, but he proves irreproachable in this regard.

Behavior: He does not very easily become friendly. He even tends to isolate himself or to show his reserve. Once he accepts the relationship, //he slowly becomes deeply involved.

You may count on him to any extent, but only as long as his position is not affected. He is very discrete.

Intellectual condition: He has a passion for intellectual discussions and abstract matters. He is knowledgeable in various fields. He knows the most varied subjects at an expert's level. He has an unbelievably profound knowledge of Romanian culture and history. He seems to have a passion for this culture: he asserts and demonstrates this by the knowledge and efforts that he displays.

Relationships: Although he has very close relationships, I believe that he is harder to influence than his superior.

Closeness and warmth of his relationships do not make him imprudent. His most important relationship in this regard is the one with his own profession.

Attitude: He is resolutely American. But he has much comprehension of foreign cultures. Regarding Romania and especially Romanian culture, he not only shows his favor, but has a clear attitude of affection. If he is correctly understood and supported, he is and will remain one of Romania's genuine friends. But the bottom line is that his attitudes are those of his government.

Conclusions: the elements of his personality are, without a doubt:

– national devotion (for America);

– tenderness in the most simple relationships;

– intellectual depth;

– sympathy for Romania (it is possible that he becomes attached in general to whatever country he is in, but it looks like Romania has won him in a special way).

Both Mr. LATHAM and his superior, Mr. McBRIDE, are personalities who bring special honor to the foreign services of the U.S.A. Both have to be appreciated as potentially favorable to Romania. Even under such circumstances that relations with them may become strained, I think these ties may be repaired again, with a degree of tact.

Within the context of relations with the U.S.A., the cultural path may play an enormous role in facilitating other aspects. In this respect, these are two people, both benevolent and extremely rational. But [appropriate] arguments are needed.

A.N.C.S.S.A., *Informative* fund, file no. 1093922, vol. I, ff. 360-363.
Handwritten indication: "The material was received on 03.18.1986".
*Underlined here and in the rest of the document.

-24-

Communication by the 3rd Directorate within D.S.S. to Special Base "T", regarding the request of video equipment for the purpose of using it for the surveillance of the diplomat Ernest Latham

Socialist Republic of Romania*

Ministry of Internal Affairs	Top Secret
MB 0625	Ex. no. 2

No. 311/L.V./D/00162554 din 19.03.1985

To Special Base "T"

Kindly make available to us a complete video kit to be used for the special action "LASCU".

The equipment will be mounted and turned to use by specialists within County Inspectorate of Iaşi of the Ministry of Internal Affairs, on 20 and 21 of March, CY.

Commander of the Base

Drawn up by L.V. / Typed by .I.S./2ex. / No.ex.R.D.230/1985

A.N.C.S.S.A., *Informative* fund, file no. 1093922, vol. IV, p. 174.

* Emblem of the R.S.R.

Handwritten indication: "I received ex. 1. / SIG, undecipherable / 03.19.1985".

-25-

Summary of notes by informer "Ionescu" regarding his relations with members of the U.S. Embassy in Bucharest, including cultural attaché Ernest Latham; characterization of the diplomat and of Romanian-American relations; "Ionescu" – "all proceedings result from the functioning rules of certain secret, omnipotent, services"; again from him – the Hungarian group in the U.S.A. operates virulently and with the aim of maintaining their advantageous positions in the American life to the detriment of the Romanians there.

S.M.B.   Top Secret

Source: "IONESCU"   Unique copy

Date: 07.18.1985

STATUS OF MY RELATIONS WITH MEMBERS OF THE U.S. EMBASSY IN BUCHAREST IN JULY 1985

A. General evolution

My connections to the American Embassy, which started approximately one year and three months ago, involved, in the order of importance, Mr. ERNEST LATHAM, cultural attaché, Mr. EDWARD McBRIDE, counsellor, Mrs. KIKI MUNSHI, director of the American Library, and Mr. MUSTAFA MUNSHI, her husband. These connections from the very beginning had a special evolution, as to their nature and in their issues. From the viewpoint of their nature, they took the shape of friendships, whether close or not, but in any rate sincere. From the viewpoint of their issues, they referred, along several steps, to the publication of several literary or theoretical works of mine in the U.S.A., a trip, a longer stay there, at the Department of Philosophy at the University of North Carolina and, finally, even if in a [...]*.

General aspects (referring to these meetings, as well as with members of the British Embassy):

– all of them ask permission for these meetings;

– the decisions on the way something is found out about the possible · course of my visits to America or England are not taken at the level of the persons I am in touch with directly; we do not have to become upset or take it personally, but slowly promote trust;

– the guidance of relationships with me (from their part) is progressively transmitted to different persons (but received from a single collaborator);

– it is obvious that all proceedings result from the rules governing the activity of powerful secret services;

– it is ridiculous to apply such rules in my case and I consider that it is done by them with too much preparatory effort; my freedom of maneuver was essential and most welcome;

– the ones I am in touch with should see a superior and positive behavior, without force;

– is this a preparation for something serious or trivial?

Referring to the long term, the prospects have evolved within a certain framework, albeit there was a crisis approximately half a year ago.

The climax was reached at the beginning of June, when everything
seemed in order concerning my one year long stay at Chapel-Hill, North
Carolina, the one and only thing still necessary being "to obtain the passport and to let the Embassy know about this". The working conditions at
the *Univ. of North Carolina* seemed excellent, there were *repeated suggestions to this effect* especially from Mr. EDWARD McBRIDE.

B. The crisis

Mr. ERNEST LATHAM was very obviously extremely satisfied
that the issue discussed by him, what he planned in general, was reaching
a positive outcome. Nevertheless, shortly before leaving for the U.S. (in
June) he seemed worried.

Difficulties arose suddenly, following two discussions, one in person and one over the phone, with Mrs. MUNSHI: it was necessary that I
be nominated by the Romanian authorities (the Ministry of Education, in
particular) for a "Fulbright" grant (discussed earlier in our relationship
and rejected by me); the only possibilities were, according to Mrs. MUN-
SHI, (a) to solve by myself the situation with our authorities or (b) *to
resume discussions with ERNEST LATHAM,* upon his return.

Mrs. MUNSHI told me she was in agreement with EDWARD
McBRIDE. With him I established a meeting, in most friendly terms,
which was then suddenly postponed, and McBRIDE suggested another
meeting (to which I could only agree after two or three days).

KIKI MUNSHI subsequently proceeded in an unexpected manner: she sent me invitations for two events at the American Library (one on July 22, followed by a reception), immediately after our discussion and much in advance, as she usually invited me almost at the last moment.

C. Reaction to the events

In the talks with KIKI MUNSHI I reacted (apparently) relaxed and understanding as to her way of presenting the matters. As I was absent from Bucharest, I did not attend the first event I had been invited to. I sent a congratulatory telegram for the 4th of July (from Neptun) to McBRIDE. I sent a few postcards from the seaside with neutral, but encouraging content.

I accidentally met on the street the Reverend of the Anglican community JOHN *KUFEN*. I did not refer to the earlier discussion, although he was aware of the previous "positive" aspects. We were to be in touch again after my return from the seaside, but it has not happened yet. I intentionally suspended my relations with the members of the British community, not wanting them to view me unfavorably and only [obtaining] their cautious support.

D. Origins of the current situation

It cannot viewed as complicated; regardless of what is problematic for them in this situation, the solution could be rather simple. There are no certainties, but seen simply, I think we have a firm point of departure, regardless of whatever assessments we may make or plausible theories we may construct.

The point of departure in the present situation is for them, as it should be for us, merely a stage, a moment of clarity in a process of full examination and of mutual appraisal and understanding. As I shall show in what follows, this *may be the best platform for launching future successes*. A scientist knows that an apparently unsuccessful experiment is likely to provide more knowledge than all the successful experiments. Maybe we will know how to turn difficulty to our advantage.

If we are not keeping pace at the moment, their failure will be interpreted as our failure, it will be alleged that we have acted strictly out of interest or even conditioned, etc.

*On their side, the difficulty is 75% real, but they are also faking it to see what happens ****.*

The hypotheses, I believe, may be reduced to four, of which two are "weak", of little power, and two "strong", of much power.

Weak hypotheses:

a) With me, they have only tried to cause a certain local destabilization, to possibly provoke some complicated reactions, to the taste of avid mass media, etc. I am sure such reactions would have been satisfactory – but I do not believe that maintaining them would have been decisive in this whole matter. None of the ones mentioned have suspected anything in this respect. Their political opinions did not prompt them to express hostile ideas towards Romania; the cultural aspect of our relationships was too important and their involvement with it, both as to information and sometimes their feelings was very clear.

This aspect did not play an important role, but they may have wanted to see in me a less stable attitude.

b) There was direct hostility against me by some of them. It could have been, for example, KIKI MUNSHI herself, a domineering person, who seldom tolerates being contradicted, which I sometimes did, to defend my own dignity. On the other hand it could have been *from the Romanians. Some of them would like to monopolize relations with the West and would do anything to eliminate competition.*

But this reason has always functioned and I do not see why it should have caused a sudden crisis – unless "my star" did not seem to rise too quick too high (especially the special and rapidly growing attention the British have shown me).

Strong interests:

a) By far the most likely alternative seems the following: they do not want a grantee there, but somebody who would *remain for good.* Several elements of discussion suggested this, even before the crisis, and especially the circumstances at the *Univ. of North Carolina,* which were probably specially organized and made attractive, but that was done to draw me into a crisis to be triggered subsequently. I suppose some were counting on me to defect.

KIKI MUNSHI, with her female intuition (and based on a previous discussion in which I told her that, unlike others, I would never have accepted just any kind of situation), rejected this alternative, as unsuitable. The transfer of the discussion to ERNEST (at the moment when McBRIDE seemed to want to control the situation) seems rather suggestive. ERNEST may be the only person able to lead the discussion along such a thorny and difficult road.

b) The second hypothesis is complementary to the first one and I consider it more a certainty than a hypothesis. The attitudes of the persons mentioned should be considered, as a whole, positive, and their present position is difficult and somewhat one sided. The definite lack of support for us – in an understanding and "mild" version – comes from the American Government. It is in this way that other failures of the relations with the U.S. should also be interpreted. This I consider to be the key to the former ambassador's behavior. If this is how things stand, it should be our duty to gain a moral advantage out of the *delicate position of these diplomats – showing our capacity of understanding, of being "hospitable", etc.*

I wonder if the former ambassador's position has not been twice distorted by elements hostile to us and maybe to America as well. Why should a special action against Romania carried out up to such a level be considered unimportant from the political viewpoint?

The U.S. is a nation dominated by national minorities. The Romanians now, as they are only at the beginning, are starting to compete with other minorities for attention there. There is no issue in America harsher than the competition among ethnic groups. The Hungarian group in the U.S. acts strongly, virulently, not only because a national conflict here would signify a modified element in the balance of the worldwide knowledge of the blocks, but also with the aim of preserving the privileged positions in the American life, to the detriment of Romanians living there. Transylvania represents also a currency capable of buying prestige on the American continent (and of undermining the prestige of Romanians living there, if possible).

While at least some of the American diplomats here are attracted by our culture and people.

E. Consequences of the situation

From the perspective of the political developments, as well as from the two bad periods, I consider I have acquired great experience in relationships of this kind, both at the behavioral level and no less at the operative level, as well as in the sphere of the moral values we are operating with.

The resulting crisis brings two advantages:

– my moral freedom versus them, a sound basis for an absolutely detached and autonomous mutual relationship, open to the assertion of my intellectual position and opinions, without any misgivings.

– here and now, for people close to me, it may be a proof of my firmness.

F. Future aspects

We shall proceed so as to make truths reveal themselves:

– we show no annoyance, no rebellion, etc.– but an attitude of superior tolerance;

– we try to transform this into a cause of concern for them, *the practical aspects will be handled with mild irony, the general cultural ones with much interest; we will try to "shelter" them, from a psychological viewpoint, from the pressures they are subjected to by their own authorities;*

– *I consider that relationships should be maintained at a frequency we cannot establish for the moment, but which should not indicate a deliberate distancing; I would aim for only one aspect:* to raise the objectives of each meeting, with respect to improving attitudes, comportment, and general atmosphere;

– *I would exercise more intensively relations with the British, and possibly with Rev. KUFEN, after it has been ascertained that it is worthwhile;*

– my relations with them should also bring to the fore their opinions: *promotion of my work in their country; what is to become of this idea if all the other ideas come from them?*

– *deeply aware that this is a difficult and delicate time, I still deem necessary to request one thing: once every month or two months it would be highly useful to invite some of them at my home (I include here the English as well). Concerning myself, nobody can influence me to make any errors anywhere. Foreigners feel deeply obliged after having been invited to one's home. Moreover, from the viewpoint of personal influence, nothing can replace this sort of meeting, in which they react by making reciprocal invitations.*

G. One little final note, I believe that this moment or stage could turn into something extremely interesting, once it unfurls to its end, or may become the prelude to a success. We have at our disposal, as a reserve and counterbalance, approximately 50 interesting connections in America and Western Europe, as well as opportunities of publication. We have started organizing a new international symposium on muscle contraction, I have a growing cultural reputation in the country.

It will be well to quickly take advantage of these travel opportunities we have (they are stirred by such events, which we have not taken advantage of lately). In case of a genuine deadlock, one should not forget that I have a censored travel book with materials regarding foreign cultures, which I can use.

I believe the greatest success of the last year and a half was the enormous growth of my power to understand and multiply experience. These are values which should not go wasted, the more so as they were acquired in often difficult circumstances.

Regardless of the current situation and whatever the explanation of facts may be, it is obvious that the functioning of their system is faulty, in spite of the enormous informational, material potential and the will they have. This is the new starting point.

A.N.C.S.S.A., *Informative* fund, file no. 1093922, vol. II, ff. 55-68.

Handwritten indication: "The material was received on 03.18.1986".

* Text underlined by the Securitate officer, accompanied by a "?".

-26-

Transcript of the recording of conversation Ernest Latham-Leon Leviţchi, at "Capşa" restaurant in Bucharest; Latham – "if you listen to the melody sung by Romania, you hear nothing – Romania has the weakest sound, the least pertinent of all East-European countries"; again him – "But as my Securist friend is saying, the revolution will come to solve everything!"

09.24.1985

SPECIAL OPERATION

LATHAM-LEVIŢCHI / "CAPŞA"

L. brought LEVIŢCHI a new edition (1984) of a book requested by LEV. during their previous meeting. It seems to be a book on a topic of geography. LEV. looks into it, then LATHAM writes an autograph for him in it! (a dedication) It is a geographic dictionary.

LEV. tells L. that the exam commission is made up of three professors, not two, as he had previously told him. *He would be one of the prof.*,* the second should be *prof. CARTIANU,* as she is v. good, although old. The other would be Mrs. *DUMITRIU (GHEORGHIŢA).* And at the final exam, the same commission would be present, *plus DAN GRIGORESCU.* L. is content with this formula.

They start talking about professional matters – L. wants to show his literary knowledge! The theme is "Suffering as a source of artistic masterpiece". L. exemplifies with ALEKSANDR SOLZHENITSYN, who was subject to great moral suffering, and consequently wrote literary masterpieces. LEV. makes no comment.

LEV. tells him to hurry up, as the exam dates have to be established as soon as possible, as he is leaving for Switzerland in Jan.-Feb., for six months.

L. thinks he will finish his paper in *December*. Then he tells LEV. that he will thus be exempted from enduring the winter here, as he will be in Switzerland. *LEV.'s daughter lives in Switzerland, she is a teacher of Engl. and French*. She is married. While in Switzerland, LEV. will continue his translation activity, he will actually revise the text, the translation is finished. He utters an exclamation referring to the difficulty of the work. L. asks him whether it is difficult to translate the work *here,* or the translation is difficult in general. LEV. says it is difficult in general, as there is a lot of bibliography.

They discuss about Switzerland in general. Then L. asks LEV. if he likes mountain climbing (!!). LEV. says he used to climb when he was younger. Then LEV. tells L. it is good that he was not in Romania in 1977, during the earthquake. He was away at that time, but their house suffered no damage, as it is a very solid building (this in relationship to the earthquake in Mexico). *Then LEV. asks L. if he speaks good Romanian, and L. confirms to him in Romanian*, because it does not seem to him a v. difficult language, the more so as he *studied Romance languages at the University*, and especially *Latin*. Hence a discussion about the Latinity of Romanian language, which L. acknowledges openly. L. eulogizes the country and the language, says he admires the Romanian people for the sense of humor, for their national hopes. It seems to him that the impact of the three great periods of influence of the three empires negatively affected the development of the country.

He says he knows of no other country being a victim of its own geographical position more so than Romania. He says he very much regrets that the politics of the last 10 centuries (?) prevented Romania from making its normal contribution to *Western* civilization, as should have happened, and as Romanians would have liked, according to his belief. LEV. does not comment. L. says the Romanian people are very talented, LEV. agrees. L. says that when our people go abroad, they realize their own value. L. very subtly says that situations and, when all is told, the extremely difficult *situation* Romania has faced over time presents a single positive aspect, namely that an *extremely* tough situation brings about a sense of the absurd and people deal with nonsense with indifference, making fun of it. He says that sometimes he thinks there is hope for the future, as national consciousness is a very powerful feeling.

LEV. says he remembers that the Dacians, our ancestors, used to weep when a child was born and to laugh when somebody was dying. L. says this way of thinking is a totally pessimistic one, while he does not look at things with pessimism. He says he sees the *world as an orchestra and each country plays the role of an instrument, and if you listen for the tune sung by Romania you hear nothing – Romania has the weakest, the least pertinent sound of all Eastern European countries.* There is no music of the pan flute, of the taragot everybody is expecting and missing. *This is why Westerners are annoyed not to hear Romania's "voice".* Then he jokes: "Let us hope that, even if you are not present for the rehearsals, you will attend the show." One of the reasons for which his work here is very interesting is the multitude, the variety of cultural life in Romania. *He then says he would very much like to be here "when Romania will start to sing again".* He also says that the Program of cultural exchanges between Rom. and the U.S. is not observed by the Romanian side. He was never able to send to the U.S. as many Romanians as he should have sent, the more so as there are many people – valuable intellectuals – who would benefit from these exchanges. For the lack of candidates from Romania, those grants are reassigned to Hungarians, Serbs, even Bulgarians. This makes him very angry, very sad. LEV. agrees people would have to learn a lot in the U.S. *L. then says: "But, as my Securist friend is saying, the revolution is going to come and solve this!"* (He feigns he is only telling it as a joke). LEV. laughs.

L. says Romania is a rich country and even from the viewpoint of the population number it would be entitled to have much more to say in this part of Europe. LEV. says Rom. is the richest in the area. L. says that before coming to take over his position he met somebody (?) in Washington who follows closely Romanian affairs and they had a long talk. He asked him, after returning from Romania, to answer a question, how is it possible for a country as rich as Romania, having at its disposal so much timber wood, so much hydroenergy, so much oil, such a long seashore, such rich land, the Danube Delta, its flourishing universities, an adequately distributed infrastructure, why this country, potentially one of the richest in Eastern Europe, should be always considered together with Albania? Now, after such a long time spent in Romania, he may affirm that Romania is truly a very rich country, offering extensive opportunities, and that there is no reason whatsoever for the current situation of Romania. The balance of Romania's natural resources is the best among the countries in Eastern Europe.

One can see that L. is waiting for a comment from LEV, but he says nothing. L. says: "O.K., that's it!...". LEV. says: "Just hope for the best."

L. adds he has spent beautiful days in Romania, he enjoyed the Romanian hospitality. His daughter, now 5, was 3 years old when she came here, now she speaks perfect Romanian – one day he was talking with his driver in Romanian and the little girl corrected him. L. is grateful to the maid who took care of his child with a sense of responsibility and love. *Then he asks LEV. directly his opinion on the situation.* Taken by surprise, LEV. answers it is a very difficult and complex issue, he cannot answer it. His philosophy regarding life is difficult. It is not easy to characterize an issue without knowing all the details, all necessary information. There are important problems, such as the atomic bomb, that seem to him much more relevant. There are psychological problems that have to be addressed.

L. says this is exactly the problem: *he himself comes from a democratic environment, in which things are "laid on the table",* in order to get the information needed and as accurate as possible insight.

L. askes LEV. how he sees the evolution of intellectual life in such difficult times. LEV. says that at present there is no more interest in the cultural act, referring, especially, to English language studies, translations, etc. There were generations of brilliant students, who had exquisite teachers.

L. asks if this lack of interest is common for all humanities.

LEV. says that, in all fields, it is sad to see that the old generation of professors, to which he also belongs, is still fighting, but without succeeding to achieve their goal, that is preserving an absolutely elementary cultural and academic posture. Before the War, French culture was predominant. After the War (...)**. He gives an example: upon the release of the "History of English and American Literature", published by "Dacia", written by him, LEV., the print run amounted to 40,000 copies, which sold immediately, but the echoes made by the book were sporadic, lacking substance.

L. asks which branches of humanities enjoy more attention. LEV.'s answer is linguistics, a domain in which CHIȚORAN published a lot, especially in the branch of (Romanian-English) quantitative analysis. *L. says he is impressed by the people working in the field of history and archeology, the more so as this area of knowledge fascinates him.* LEV. acknowledges that much has been done regarding history. Different theories have been dispelled, as well as rumors, etc., while "Magazin Istoric" is a very serious publication. L. says he knows this magazine to be widely popular. IORGA is for him a fascinating personality, he just bought a (reprinted) book written by him.

L. says he recently gave a talk on Romanian culture to American citizens. He made the observation that every book published in Romania between 1920 and 1940 was written by N. IORGA, and if it was not written by him, at least the preface was by him (probably concerning the books of history). Or if the preface was not by him, at least it was dedicated to him. LEV. says that while he was himself a student in Letters and Philosophy, everybody was fascinated by IORGA. The lecture rooms were always overcrowded. His only flaw was he made lots of digressions, jumping from one subject to the next. L. is interested if he knew him in person. LEV. answers yes, he was a very kind man. L. says it is a pity he had such a tragic end. Then L. says he does not understand why it happened this way, knowing that IORGA was a great nationalist, why should the legionaries kill him? LEV. says yes, there was a short period, but IORGA was a democrat, he could not agree with the legionaries.

L. says there were other fascinating personalities in the epoch, some of whom are no longer mentioned – one example being NAE IONESCU. LEV. remembers him, but did not meet him. GEORGE CĂLINESCU was a great man of letters. L. has the "History of Literature" written by him. LEV. says he made a translation of this masterpiece, to be published soon. It is a monumental work, he worked tremendously to accomplish it, only the quoted poem lines amount to 11,000. The publication is to be made in Milano. L. asks why it is published in Milano and not England or the U.S. LEV. says it is so probably because the English or Americans are not interested.

L. is interested to know if the recent reissue of the "History of Literature" includes changes, essential modifications, referring, mainly, to the ones with an ideological content. LEV. says that, *as far as he knows,* there are no ideological changes, but in the area of biographies – years, locations (data), titles, translations, etc.

L. says this is encouraging.

L. says he read CĂLINESCU's comments regarding NAE IO-NESCU (he certainly has the 1940 edition of the "History of Literature", as he does not know whether the chapter still exists in the republished version!). LEV. says that CĂLINESCU criticized IORGA in his work. *He also wrote about a certain EMIL CIORAN – a philosopher he also criticized.*

L. invites LEV. to have some more, but he refuses him, says he has had enough. L. asks LEV. if it is convenient to him to meet for lunch, or he would prefer dinner. LEV. says it does not bother him, any hour is fine.

L. says the date of the exams should be established, and LEV. tells him he has to finish urgently the two chapters of the paper! *L. says they have a difficult issue with the computers at the office*, but suggests they should meet as soon as possible again, for lunch, when he will give him the texts. LEV. agrees and tells him repeatedly: "The sooner, the better for both of us!" The dates for the exams would be settled taking into account LEV.'s departure. L. says he may leave for the U.S. for Christmas. L. says he will give him the two chapters, approximately 15 pages long, each of them. LEV. tells him to make a summary of the two chapters. Anyway, the entire paper should be about 200 pages. LEV. explains how the paper should be drawn up, how to speak during the exam, how the exam will unfold.

It seems that the final exam will be next year, in August, and LEV. wonders, will L. stay so long? L. says he is not certain, but *has the impression he would stay two more years here! He very much hopes so.* If he does not succeed to stay, he will make arrangements to return from time to time, he will send the chapters, and will take part in person in the exams. LEV. suggests the end of October for the first exam and end of Nov. for the last two. They write down in their calendars (therefore, Oct. 24 and Nov. 15).

The two thank each other for the company and leave the restaurant.

Rendition from English: CPT. SIG. HUSZAR

A.N.C.S.S.A., *Informative* fund, file no. 1093922, vol. IV, ff. 211-215.

* Underlined here and in the rest of the document.

Resolution: "Leaving aside the issues connected to the doctorate, the discussion actually reflects the diplomat's true opinions on the realities in our country. / Check if and how the professors on the commission are known and set out in a timely manner the briefing of the ones who are sources. When the diplomat will look for them, they should already be prepared, in order to make his informative exploitation (as well as of his interest) part of his thorough profile. / SIG, undecipherable".

** Text interrupted in the original.

-27-

Report of Bureau III within the County Inspectorate Bihor of the Ministry of Internal Affairs, to the 3rd Directorate within D.S.S.,
regarding the results of surveillance of the
diplomat Ernest Latham in the county, on September 30, 1985

Socialist Republic of Romania*	Top Secret
Ministry of Internal Affairs	Ex. no. 1
County Inspectorate Bihor / Securitate / Bureau III	
No. 310/BT/0088063/Oct. 7, 1985	

To the Ministry of Internal Affairs / Department of State Security
3rd Directorate / Bucharest

[REPORT]

Following your phone order, we report that on 09.30.1985 the cultural counsellor ERNEST LATHAM from the U.S. Embassy in Bucharest was in Oradea in order to be present during the unpacking of boxes containing art objects brought from Vienna for the American exhibition to be opened on 10.08.1985, at the Museum of Țara Crișurilor in Oradea.

As a result of the information and operative proceedings undertaken in connection with the visit of the American diplomat, we have established the following:

– ERNEST LATHAM arrived on the first flight, and was met by AVRAM VASILE, son of Constantin and Maria, born 01.12.1925, in Homoreni, Suceava, domiciled in Bucharest, str. I.B. Tito no. 21, Sector 3. It was established he had arrived in Oradea one day earlier and is the permanent representative of the U.S. Embassy for the duration of the exhibition.

The two of them witnessed the opening of the packages, together with the director of the Museum and the Customs representative, and everything developed normally. Afterwards, ERNEST LATHAM was guided by the director of the Museum and the chiefs of departments through the Museum, and was shown the rooms to host the exhibition and the opening festivities.

The cultural attaché returned to Bucharest on the same day, on the 19.00 hours flight.

ERNEST LATHAM conveyed the Embassy's wish for the opening of the exhibition to be attended by as many physicians as possible.

With respect to the American exhibition, we have established its organizing at the Museum of Ţara Crişurilor as well has been proposed by the Council of Culture – the Department of Foreign Cultural Relations.

Two weeks ago, OLGA MANIU from the U.S. Embassy in Bucharest requested the lists of protocol and the time for the opening of the exhibition, in order to mention on the poster the Embassy's guests as well.

As a result of the information and operative proceedings undertaken, the inclusion *on the protocol list of persons with negative manifestation was prevented***, therefore on it are officials and persons who frequently visit exhibitions, creators of fine art, museologists, journalists, directors of enterprises, etc.

After receiving the list, OLGA MANIU called again the management of the Museum and noted that the list did not include the mayor of the Municipality, other officials on the County and Municipal Committee of the P.C.R., representatives of the U.T.C. and the religious denominations, especially the Baptists, insisting for them to be invited as well. At the same time, cultural attaché *ERNEST LATHAM insisted that the representatives of the religions in Oradea to be invited as well.* Representatives of the denominations will be invited upon agreement of the party authorities.

OLGA MANIU offered to sell to the chief of the Arts Section of the Museum l certain personal artworks, inviting her to visit her home in order to see the objects. The latter directed her to the Museum of Art in Bucharest, but upon Mrs. MANIU's insistence, she promised to pay her a visit, out of courtesy.

Concerning the artistic value of the exhibits, the artists assess the exhibition as not being anything special as compared to other exhibitions, even commented negatively that the value of the works of art sent over does not surpass the usual art production level in any country.

Moreover, they have sent over three very heavy pieces (sculptures), while it is customary to only send (small size) salon sculpture.

We confirm we have undertaken complex steps of surveillance of the Embassy's representatives during their stay in Oradea, for the opening of the exhibition.

We will follow up.

Chief of Securitate, colonel, SIG, SIMA TRAIAN***

Chief of Bureau III, colonel, SIG, ARONESCU C-TIN

A.N.C.S.S.A., *Informative* fund, file no. 1093922, vol. II, p. 93.

Handwritten indications: 1) "S.1"; 2) B.1/L.V. / Extract the aspects concerning OLGA MANIU – material to be examined. / SIG, undecipherable"; 3) "V./R.".

* Emblem of the R.S.R.

** Underlined here and in the rest of the document.

*** Seal of the respective military base

-28-

Report of the recording of a conversation between the diplomats Ernest Latham and Melanie Munshi, in hotel "Astoria" in Oradea

311/L.V.   Top Secret

Ex. no. 1

SPECIAL OPERATION

HOTEL "ASTORIA" – ORADEA – 10.07.1985 – 22.00

KIKI MUNSHI WAS LODGED IN ROOM 107, LATHAM ERNEST IN ROOM 109

After KIKI remarks it is very dark outside, LATHAM asks how many bottles [of wine] were sent to the reception. KIKI says enough bottles were sent, as she told the people to be generous, taking into consideration the reception will be attended by approximately 150 persons. She speaks about the way sandwiches will be served and what kind of sandwiches, although she thinks that the public is not really interested in food on such occasions.

KIKI asks whether there is a list of guests and LATHAM says the list is in Bucharest, but he knows them by heart. Then KIKI says the weather is splendid. LATHAM agrees, then brings out his passport and examines the way the Hungarian stamp was applied. Then says he has the passport since he was accredited to Romania. KIKI says her passport must add some pages, in order to make room for the extension of stay in Romania. LATHAM has to do this as well. KIKI then asks when and where he let his moustache grow. LATHAM says during the first assignment, in Cyprus.

KIKI says that, unlike LATHAM, she drove very many kilometers with her own car, since she is in Romania.

The two of them then discuss about landscapes in Pennsylvania. LATHAM recounts about a very nice party he attended when he went to the U.S., when only champagne was served. Hence, a dialogue on wines and champagne.

KIKI then says she has to plan carefully her holidays, in order to be able to travel in as many places as possible. LATHAM already finished his vacation, part of which he spent together with KAREN.

KIKI remembers KAREN is going to come here in the first two weeks of November and tells LATHAM she asked RONA PAZDRAL on the availability of the transit apartment, but she said it was too early to know the situation. KIKI suggests to bring KAREN to the "Marines'

Ball", to take place on a Saturday, November 8 or 9, she does not know for sure on what day it is. KIKI thinks she will be a duty officer that day and will not participate. She does not know for sure, but thinks it will be this way and asks LATHAM when he will have the duty, as she follows after LATHAM. Neither is LATHAM aware. He remembers that in November he is to stand for some exams for his doctor's degree. KIKI asks him how things go, and what he settled with LEVIȚCHI, concerning the doctorate. LATHAM explains the procedure, how he will organize his work, what subject he has chosen. They discuss different American authors – novelists –, especially about HENRY JAMES and then STEPHEN CRANE.

LATHAM then says the girlfriend of a friend of his died […]* last year. Speaking of […], KIKI says a "Fulbright" grantee […] has been operated on. A nice girl, she was about to get married. LATHAM remembers that VAN HORN is training in the field of commerce. He was working a lot with TONY PARKER. KIKI says it looks like TONY is very happy. He is here again…

Then they speak about MERRY BLOCKER, who was also friend of CHRIS VAN HORN's. Speaking of MERRY BLOCKER, KIKI says she received a telegram from MARY ANN IGNATIUS, who told her that BLOCKER was very content in Argentina. At the same time, she learned from somebody else who was in Argentina that MERRY BLOCKER would like to leave the Foreign Service. LATHAM is surprised, knowing that MERRY was enthusiastic about Argentina, while being herself a very able person, able to go through thick and thin. KIKI says she is convinced MERRY worked a lot there as well, as she did here, but probably she could no longer resist. LATHAM says he cannot realize what had happened. MERRY has an outstanding personality, an exceptional talent for this work, but was not very appreciated, especially due to the fact that she constantly aimed at emphasizing her merits. KIKI says that, as far as she is concerned, MERRY never tried to impress her. LATHAM recounts that once, in Washington, he met her and her sister and a friend of hers – ADAM. They talked, mainly about Romania, and MERRY started boasting about what she had done here. Then they went to a reception, and MERRY continued along the same line, until, at a moment, he felt awkward.

Then they discuss about a future location for the exhibition – namely Craiova, and KIKI asks what area this place is close to, and LATHAM says it is close to Yugoslavia and they both laugh. KIKI asks LATHAM if he travelled extensively in Czechoslovakia, and he says not much, and only by train. He only saw Prague. KIKI starts humming a few bars from a song, probably Czechoslovakian. LATHAM asks if she went to Prague in 1968. She remembers the city very well. She was there immediately after August 1968, in September. She liked it very much and would like to go back there.

KIKI asks him if he wants to return to his room or wants "to have an argument" – or believes that the place is not quite appropriate. LATHAM believes it is not quite appropriate. KIKI agrees. Then LATHAM goes and opens the window – they go to speak at the window and nothing more is heard.

Then KIKI asks something (I do not understand what) and they probably move to some other place, as the exchange is heard from far away. The noise of the street increased, and their voices heard from a distance. I guess they are at the window, looking out. After closing the window, they return to their initial places. LATHAM asks her if she wants one more drink, KIKI says no. Then they say "good bye" and "good night". KIKI remains alone in the room. She is heard searching through her things, then the recording ends.

L.V./I.S./2 ex. / R.D.1258/1985

A.N.C.S.S.A., *Informative* fund, file no. 1093922, vol. IV, ff. 222-223.

Handwritten indication: "Ex. 2 I.S.D. *MELANIA*".

* Here and further down in the document, aspects regarding private life are not published.

–29–

Communication of Bucharest Municipality Securitate to 3rd Directorate a D.S.S. transmitting a note regarding statements of the diplomat Ernest Latham on Romanian-American relations; Latham – "Romanian-American relations will continue to be under pressure on the human rights issue"; he "trusts the talent and capacity of the Romanian people to overcome some difficult moments"

Socialist Republic of Romania*	Top Secret
Ministry of Internal Affairs	Ex. no. 1

Department of State Security / Bucharest Municipality Securitate

122/D.I./0070209/12.05.1985

To the 3rd Directorate,

Find attached, for the purpose of exploitation, the copy of a note referring to certain comments made by LATHAM E.**, cultural attaché at the U.S. Embassy in Bucharest, on the occasion of the opening of the American photography exhibition at the Museum of the R.S.R.

Chief of Securitate, General-Major BUCURESCU GIANU, SIG***

Chief of Bureau, CPT CREȚA STANA, SIG

Typing: 373/3150/N.M.

[Annex]

NOTE

On Nov. 15, during the opening of the American photography exhibition at the Museum of the R.S.R., I had a conversation with LATHAM E., cultural attaché of the U.S. Embassy. On this occasion, referring to the arrival of a new American ambassador in Bucharest, he said that his mission will be a highly complex one, because "today Romania is, more than ever, under the scrutiny of U.S. public opinion. Never before, – he stated, – was there such a marked interest in the U.S. concerning Romania", which he considered, from this point of view, together with the Soviet Union and Poland.

He pointed out he was convinced Romanian-American relations will continue to be under pressure because of human rights issues, an issue which, in his opinion, will be key to American attitude concerning bilateral cooperation. He admitted, at the same time, that there are no burning issues in this area, adding that the resolution of such cases as those of DORIN TUDORAN and priest CALCIU are viewed positively.

As concerns the future development of commercial relations, especially the granting of the most favored nation clause, he mentioned that besides the sentiment to maintain this status, believing that this may avoid both a decline of political relations and negative impact on the Romanian economic situation, there are great doubts; however, as to what extent the profile of investments made, by virtue of financial facilities, has subsequent favorable effects on the Romanian-American exchanges or on establishing a trade balance.

He emphasized that, from his viewpoint, he trusts the talent and capacity of the Romanian people to overcome some difficult moments, and that, taking into consideration the country's resources, he anticipates the growth of the Romanian economy in the next two or three years.

A.N.C.S.S.A., *Informative* fund, file no. 1093922, vol. II, ff. 133-134.

Handwritten indication at the beginning of the document: "B.1".

* Emblem of the R.S.R.

** In the document and annex: "LOTMAN F."

*** Seal of the respective institution.

-30-

Report signaled by MB 0672/Bucharest, to the 3rd Directorate within D.S.S., regarding a meeting of diplomat Ernest Latham with Caius Dragomir, at "Capşa" restaurant

Ministry of Internal Affairs	Top Secret
Department of State Security	Unique copy
MB 0672 / Bucharest	
No. D/005473537 of 01.31.1986	

To the 3rd Directorate / Indicative 311

REPORT

On 01.28.1986, between 13.00-15.20, target "LASCU", cultural attaché at the U.S. Embassy, had lunch at "Capşa" restaurant with a person later left at str. Dr. Iatropol no. 24, villa-type house (who is being identified).

Specific action was taken at the restaurant by the intelligence unit.*

In the annex is a photograph of the target with the mentioned person.**

Deputy Base commander, Col., SIG, undecipherable***

Chief of Bureau, col., SIG, undecipherable

Drafted by B.G./12/14

[Annex]

[„LASCU" (1) şi C. DRAGOMIR]

A.N.C.S.S.A., *Informative* fund, file no. 1093922, vol. II, p. 172.

Handwritten indication at the beginning of document: "B.1/L.V.".

* Handwritten indication: "Yes".

** Handwritten indication: "CAIUS DRAGOMIR". The indication is confirmed by the following note and identification of MB 0672 Bucharest no. D/00473500 dated January 30, 1986 (same file, vol. II, p. 180).

*** Seal of the respective military base.

-31-

Transcript of the recorded conversation of Ernest Latham, Melanie Munshi, and Silviu Brucan,
at "Capşa" restaurant in Bucharest; the meanings of the ballad "Miorița"; Brucan – "the
American's granting the clause did not help the
Romanian people much"; again him – Romanian
intellectuals are desperate and wait for a
change, the idea of a global change is the only
hope; Brucan wants American pressure on the
Romanians in his case – a "test-case"

02.19.1986

SPECIAL OPERATION – "CAPŞA" REST.

KIKI MUNSHI – K.

LATHAM – L.

SILVIU BRUCAN – B.

B. says they will discuss first the translation, then about different opinions on it. L. agrees.

The three of them discuss the translation made by L. and K. The text in question is the poem (ballad) "Miorița". The two of them asked B.'s opinion on it. The latter says his wife is literature-savvy and she read the translation and likes it.

Then, the conversation evolves around the translation. BRUCAN offers suggestions to the two diplomats. They discuss the philosophical meanings of the ballad, with reference to the analysis made by BLAGA on the philosophic significance of the ballad.

Afterwards, B. says that the Congress of C.P.S.U., to occur soon, is expected to announce certain changes in the labor legislation and the income of working people in the U.S.S.R. A lot was written on this subject *lately and everybody expects to see what will come out of this. K. says that probably the other socialist countries will follow the example, and B. says that anyway our country will be the last to follow this example!** The other countries may follow it. An issue that is now drawing a lot of attention in U.S.S.R. is increasing the quality of services. For example, articles were written on a technical repair workshop in Georgia, which is famous for the quality and promptness of its work, and as a consequence the staff's monthly income has doubled. Russian newspapers provided more such examples, and this shows that that branch of activity will be encouraged. The idea is that workers' income will be no longer limited, but the first criterion considered will be quality of their work. B. quotes a few opinions on this subject made by DENG XIAOPING (China's leader), asserting that he and all Chinese, are methodical.

LATHAM adds that they are nationalistic and xenophobic as well. Russians, on the other hand, are very sentimental. B. says Chinese do not have a sense of humor, but they work diligently, just as the Japanese do.

Then B. starts narrating that M. BOTEZ wrote a very interesting book, on the history of Romanian-American relations**. L. asks if the book was published here and B. says it was not published here, suggesting it was published somewhere else. He starts describing the subject of the book, showing it follows two lines: one indicating Romanian-American relations followed an ascending tendency, up to the point of NIXON's visit and the visits of the Romanian president to the U.S. It is then observed that the American granting the clause did not help the Romanian people much. L. asks whether this is true. B. says that, from the logical viewpoint, it is true. L. then asks what should have been done. B. says he will return to his opinion, after presenting the whole of BOTEZ's idea. *BOTEZ says that Romanian intellectuals are discontent at the moment and, even if in the past they were for the regime, they are now waiting for a change. B. says this is true,* because intellectuals are desperate and, even if the idea of a global change does not please them, this is the only hope. K. agrees with him.

Upon L.'s question, he gives the following answer: in his view, the Romanian people went through three stages: the first stage was subordination to the Soviets, when history was re-written in order to accord with the theory that the Romanian people are of Slavic origin. Then came the second stage, in the latter part of the 1960s, when an opposite movement occurred, just as extreme as the first one, and Russian culture was excluded – no more Russian literature of value was translated or published – TOLSTOY, DOSTOYEVSKY etc. At present, there is a trend of renewed interest in Soviet culture: movies, ballet.

K. asks B. if he received an invitation to the journalist's conference. B. says he did not. He discussed it with friends and none did. K. promises to send him an invitation and asks if he prefers it to be sent to his house. B. says it is better to invite him by phone, as the traffic in the area where he lives is restricted to cars belonging to persons residing in the area (str. Herăstrău 16).

L. asks why taxis no longer circulate. B. says they were interrupted for economic reasons. L. says tourists have no means of transport. B. says that if they pay in dollars, they may use hotel services. L. considers such a measure does not encourage tourism. B. says it is in nobody's interest, but nevertheless it is enforced!

B. comes back to the initial subject – the discussion referring to "Miorița". He says the main controversy concerning "Miorița" is among BLAGA, DAN BOTTA, MIRCEA ELIADE, and HENRI STAHL. The latter is one of the pioneers of Romanian sociology, an old man – 80 years old, but very good. He is DIMITRIE GUSTI's disciple. B. explains to the diplomats the differences of a philosophical nature among the above mentioned.

LATH. asks B. if, taking into consideration what he saw of the translation, as well as what they told him about the "Miorița" exhibition, this could in any way annoy the Romanian authorities. B. says this is a form of flattering, not an insult. L. insists with his question, wanting to know if opening a subject considered closed, such as "Miorița", anyone could consider this inappropriate. B. says he did not consider this aspect, there may exist persons thinking this way. L. says he asked the question because they he had been that very day at the Council of Culture and asked if they could borrow some objects of folk art for the exhibition. He had the impression his question caused a certain nervousness. B. says that in his opinion he should combine Romanian elements and effective support from Romanian specialists, with the ones in the American Library. B. suggests for the Institute of Ethnography to be engaged in the project.

L. says he discussed with LAZĂR and CIUBUNZU at the Council. LAZĂR does duty for ILEASĂ. B. knows LAZĂR, who was active in diplomacy. He labels him as not outstandingly intelligent, but this looks as a factor in his selection. The diplomats laugh. B. says that, logically speaking, nobody should have anything against the subject of the exhibition, but logic is a bourgeois element! The diplomats laugh.

B. says he has learned that hearings have started in the Senate regarding suspending the clause for Romania. Then says he does not expect this step to be effective, but one never knows. L. agrees to the last remark. B. says that, as far as he knows, the opinion in Senate and Congress is not favorable to Romania. L. says it will not be easy. B. says that, in this *respect, he discussed with his friends in the M.F.A. and they told him that they also have to have the approval of the higher leadership for what they are going to do or say. This because with us, Romanians, [the principle] is that state officials should be very careful not to anger the ones "high above". This is why they do not consider that the problems, the reasons are important enough to be reported to the superior leader-ship.*

B. also says all his friends are following very closely his case, con-sidering it a test-case. If they can stop him (stop B.), then it means they will be able to do it with anybody! Under the circumstances, his case is "representative". Two years ago there was the same situation and FUN-DERBURK went to the M.F.A. and within 24 hours he received his pass-port. Eventually, the ones in charge will be obliged to upset the "ones high above" and communicate to them his case. L. says FUNDERBURK did not discuss with the higher leadership, with ȘT. ANDREI, therefore the issue could be solved at the lower level. B. says there were then two lines of intervention, one through ED. DARWINSKI, who was in the country at the time and the other through the U.S. Embassy, FUNDER-BURK, to ANDREI. If these two levels of intervention are utilized, his problem will not be known "high up".

L. says that, in his opinion, B. should hope, because *they (the Amer-icans) have moved the "field of activity" from Bucharest to Washington. DASH is in a position to instruct the ones in the Embassy, and also to put pressure on Romanian authorities.* B. says this depends on them.

L. says that B. is a person known in the U.S. He also says that there is a certain irony in the situation: taking into consideration B.'s present and his past position, how is this possible? (He refers to B.'s past position in the party.) B. insists that it is only through the two channels indicated by him that his case may come to the attention of superior party leader-ship. L. says it would be more effective *to apply a double pressure.* On the one hand through the ambassador, who would thus assume the risk of being told he should mind his own business. B. says the ambassador should mention his intervention is made in the name of Romania's inter-ests, in the name of the clause. The American position is very good and they can make it. All that counts is to reach a high level, which has not been done so far. Through the American Secretary of State, there is a way to reach to the secretary general. LATH. says this issue, of reaching to the top, is extremely difficult, they permanently face it. *B. says the clause should be [invoked], which is vital for Romania.*

K. asks B. if he is sure that only acting along these two channels a positive solution to his case can be achieved. B. answers affirmatively. Then she asks him if he knows for sure that at the lower level no important decision is taken. B. again answers affirmatively. K. asks what sort of decisions are taken at the M.F.A. level. B. says only simple issues are approved, they do not take responsibilities. L. asks why the superior leadership does not want to hear this bad news (regarding him). B. says this is not bad news, if it is properly presented. They have heard much worse news in the past! Much more serious cases! The priest and the writer (CALCIU and TUDORAN) caused them many more headaches and still they let them go! His case is not as difficult.

L. asks why the M.F.A. people do not want to report the situation. B. says they are not doing it because they are afraid of the reaction of the persons above, that they will get angry. L. says they would be even angrier if the news came from Washington. B. confirms he is right, but he personally cannot do anything. The Embassy has to make this point. L. says they have tried to, but did not accomplish anything. *B. says he knows for sure that the person in charge of his case has asked whether to prepare a report to be forwarded "up there", and the answer was "no".*

B. also says that in 1978 a team of economic experts came over who established, on the basis of data presented by Romanian authorities, that there is a great discrepancy between the industrialization projects and their economic potential. They wanted to caution the people concerned about this. At the ministry, they were told to mind their own business, because otherwise the superior leadership would get furious. L. says the results may be seen now! He adds the situation is "dramatic, to say the least"! B. says that what is more dramatic is that in the future things will not be better, but worse. B. says that, in his opinion, the Americans are interested to maintain the clause, under certain conditions. L. agrees. B. says that, at present, the condition is represented by the pressure wielded by Congress. He also says that, *while Soviet-American relations are warming up, the American conservatives direct their attacks against Romania, as they need a political debate.* L. does not agree with this.

B. insists, saying he has read the report concerning the situation of human rights in Romania and has seen the very critical tone. L. contradicts him, saying that Romanian-American relations do nevertheless follow an ascending line. B. says that one of the correct assessments found by him in BOTEZ's book is that the lack of economic efficiency, bringing about the current internal situation, put Romania at the Soviet's mercy. Romania needs oil and coal, and the only place it can get it from is the U.S.S.R. L. says the cost is very high! Romania's independence, so much under discussion, if analyzed at the economic level, is extremely fragile! Romanians have played a difficult role and the only thing they may do is to trust both positions. L. also says that losing M.F.N. would mean as much as losing the trust from the Americans and, at the same time, opening the possibility of a Soviet intervention in Romania's economic plans.

B. says he agrees with him. He has carefully read KIRK's speech, who strongly opposed the idea of withdrawing the clause. He said that other aspects must be taken into consideration. L. says he does not believe that suspending it for 6 months, as recommended, would serve both sides. B. says the Americans have many efficient means of convincing the Romanians of this fact. L. says that attempts were made, without any success. B. says that in the meeting he is not allowed to attend 1,500 personalities will participate and if the president of the said association were to announce that the vice-president (namely B.) could not make it because the Romanian authorities would not allow him to come, this would produce a huge outcry. This could be an argument for the Romanians. L. says that here this is not an argument, because here it does not matter what happens in the U.S. This is why actions, pressures, should be made both here and in the U.S.

In the end, B. agrees with LATH.

The discussion takes an end.

Rendered from English by CPT HUSZAR

A.N.C.S.S.A., *Informative* fund, file no. 1093922, vol. IV, ff. 330-334.

Handwritten indication: "ERNEST LATHAM, first secretary in charge with cultural matters / MELANIE MUNSHI – attaché".

* Underlined here and in the rest of the document.

** Handwritten indication: "Serial *Free Europe*".

-32-

Note by informer "Oprea", given to resident "Cătălin", regarding the activity of diplomats Ernest Latham and Melanie Munshi; checking and recruiting employees at the old book stores in the center of Bucharest; the Romanian women employed at the U.S. Embassy have requested food supplies from the mission.

311/L.V.   Top Secret

Source "OPREA"   Unique copy

02.26.1986

[NOTE]

On 02.11 I went to "Intercontinental" hotel, took Prof. DARWELL and brought him to the Library, where he had a conference, followed by a reception, then brought him back to the hotel.

On 02.12. I went with KIKI and DARWELL for lunch at the residence of Mexico's ambassador, then KIKI told me to take them to *Unirii Square, where they got out of the car, at the church "Domniţa Bălaşa", then went to the former prison Văcăreşti, where they looked from the car, afterwards I took them to the Embassy**. KIKI remained at the Emb., and LATHAM accompanied him to the airport.

On 02.17 I took STROVAS to the ambassador's residence, for a reception, then back to Emb.

On 02.18. I took LATHAM to A.D.I.R.I. for a meeting, and then to "Muzica" shop, where he bought records of GHEORGHE ZAMFIR's and to the *"Anticariatul" at the Palace**, where he bought books.*

On 02.19. I took LATHAM and OLGA MANIU to a meeting at the Council of Culture and Socialist Education.

On 02.21. I took LATHAM to the airport, where Prof. HAMMER was expected to arrive, from Vienna, but only his luggage came, he had missed the flight. LATHAM told me to wait for him on Sunday, at 19.15, he was not going to come to the airport.

On 02.24. I am supposed to take HAMMER from "Intercontinental" hotel, at 08.20, and bring him to the Emb.

At 9.40 HAMMER and STROVAS for meeting at "Şt. Gheorghiu" Academy, at 14.00 meeting at A.D.I.R.I.

On 02.25., 10.15 HAMMER from "Intercontinental" together with STROVAS and LATHAM for meeting at the Institute of Historical and Social-Politic Studies, to Mr. POPESCU-PUŢURI.

At 12.15 from Emb. To the ambassador's residence, and then, 15.15, to the airport.

Addition:

At the former prison Văcărești they asked the source to stop on Șoseaua Olteniței (in the back), where there is a breach in the fence and the interior can be seen. They stayed in the car and talked (source did not understand), without stepping down.

On Sunday, Prof. HAMMER will be awaited by CARMEN CONSTANTINESCU.

At the Consulate, certain changes were made in the way watch is organized. The marines who had stayed in the waiting room will now stay in the hall (where AUREL LUPAȘCU stayed until now). For AUREL they will build a booth outside and another person (a Romanian) will be hired also for watch.

CARMEN CONSTANTINESCU told the source the black lady will no longer come to replace EDWARDS, she had resigned. KIKI will stay one more year, at the Library, and the person who was to replace KIKI in a year will take over EDWARDS's position.

GIGI ANTON told him that, at the Press Section, GETA CIOCÂLTEA will be replaced by an employee who now works in the Commercial branch of the Embassy (RODA, probably).

CARMEN CONSTANTINESCU told the source that Romanian employees *(OLGA, BETY, RODICA RADU, OLIVIA) requested they should be provided foodstuffs (meat, especially) through the Embassy, but STROVAS did not approve, because, according to him, "it is not legal".* At the same time, they requested from STROVAS that when private automobile traffic is prohibited they should have a car to bring them home; this request was not approved, either.

Source daily brings the news (in the morning), to the Min. of Foreign Affairs in 7 copies, T.V. 1, "Agerpres" 1, "Scânteia" 1, "R. Liberă" 1, C.C. of the P.C.R. 3.

"CĂTĂLIN"

N.L.

Through the officer in charge with the Library Center, we will acquire the data of all employees working in the "Anticariate" in the central area of the Capital (Kretzulescu, B-dul Magheru, Curtea Domnească), as well as of the ones working in the Center for collecting books from private providers.

All of them will be examined and we will recruit sources out of their number – in order to keep under observation though them the activity of the American diplomats who visit them.

At the same time, I will carry out the recruitment, as a collaborator, of the employee at Dorobanți old books store.

The data referring to HAMMER will be exploited in Notes to the higher echelon. Information about KIKI MUNSHI, as well as about Romanian employees, will be exploited in their files.

The source will continue to keep us informed about LATHAM's and KIKI's links.

MJR LAZĂR VALERIU

A.N.C.S.S.A., *Informative* fund, file no. 1093922, vol. II, ff. 199-100.

Handwritten indication at the beginning of the document: "I.S.D. LASCU".

* Underlined here and in the rest of the document.

** Handwritten indication: "Kretzulescu".

-33-

Communication of Securitate of Bucharest Municipality to 3rd Directorate within D.S.S., in order to forward the note of informer "Leon" referring to Ernest Latham; "Leon" – Latham in disagreement with the social-politic system in R.S.R., but very attached to the "infrastructure of Romanian people"; the case officer – "certainly a C.I.A. officer"

Ministry of Internal Affairs   Top Secret

Securitate of Bucharest Municipality   Ex. no. 1

No. 160/MB/0054890/03.28.1986

To the 3rd Directorate / Col. GH. DIACONESCU

Find attached a briefing, to be exploited,

referring to ERNEST LATHAM, counsellor at the U.S. Embassy.

Chief of Securitate, general-major, SIG, undecipherable*

Chief of Bureau, Lt. Col. URECHE MARIAN, SIG

373/468 / N.M.**

[Annex]

03.18.1986

NOTE REGARDING ERNEST HARGREAVES LATHAM JUNIOR, CULTURAL ATTACHÉ AT THE U.S. EMBASSY, BUCHAREST

Mr. LATHAM, PhD candidate in the history of American literature (subject of dissertation: "Oliver Wendell Holmes, tradition and innovation in his outlook on history" – HOLMES, 1809-1894, writer and *well-known physician), often engaged in conversation with me in the period February 1985-January 1986, as I am his dissertation supervisor*** (at the recommendation of the Ministry of Education and the Rector).

What follows *represents moments from dialogues we had during receptions, at "Capşa", where he invited me about 5 or 7 times* and in our home (I invited him to a Romanian dinner, 01.27.1986, together with his daughter, CHARLOTTE, 5 and a half years old).

Biographical data

He has been in the American Diplomatic Service for 11 years, in regions close to Turkey (Cyprus, for example). Coming from Boston, he studied humanities in the university (Latin, Greek). He has a remarkable culture, knows very *well the history*, culture, and literature of the Romanian people, using for his documentation the *Romanian language* as well, for which he has sufficient knowledge. He shows an outstanding interest in this area and I understand he is teaching these subjects to Americans in Washington or Bucharest.

I do not know whether he is divorced or a widower. *He has two children, CHARLOTTE and an 11 year old boy*, who is in Washington. He is taking extreme care of the girl's education and, *regardless if he will be appointed or not again in Bucharest,* he would like her to learn in Romania (for the time being, she is enrolled at the French kindergarten).

The relationship between father and daughter is impressively affectionate.

He confessed to me he would very much like to stay longer in Romania (it was not clear if this fact, as well as his PhD, would facilitate for him a promotion in diplomacy).

He brilliantly passed the two compulsory exams (commission: ANA CARTIANU, GETA DUMITRIU, myself – Nov. 1985), as well as two papers (in front of the members of the English Literature Chair in my former department – January 1986).

Attitudes

He does not agree with *our social-political system,* but he (unlike his predecessors at the American Embassy) feels very attracted by what he calls "infrastructure of the Romanian people" (traditions, Latin continuity, national specificity, culture, art, character, hospitality). He stressed on several occasions that Americans and Westerners, in general, do not know the real role played by Romania along the centuries in this part of Europe and that we, Romanians, do not make for ourselves sufficient publicity in the Occident, unlike the Hungarians. He gladly accepted my suggestion for him to send invitations for the Congress of American Studies in Budapest (March 1986) to professors DINU GIURESCU and SEVER TRIFU (Cluj), in order for them to *counter the possible Hungarian interventions to our detriment* (the congress is also dealing with historical issues, even if only ones connected to the U.S. during the Revolution).

He believes that the "truth must come to light", speaking of the part played by Romania during World War II, because it is a mistake for Romania not to be considered a belligerent state by the Allies, it is not true that Jews were persecuted by Marshal ANTONESCU (a very mistaken opinion held today in the U.S.) or that Marshal ANTONESCU was a fascist or a pro-fascist. Let me mention Mr. LATHAM is a sincere Protestant and is not anti-Semitic.

Personal opinions

Mr. LATHAM is one of the few *"true-born" Americans who are on our side in the disputes with the Hungarians, because he has thoroughly studied our history* (along the years, I have met enough Americans hostile to us). *He gives me the impression of a humanist, objective and sensitive intellectual.*

[N.O.]

– Source from S.M.B. has written before such notes on LATHAM for Serv. 6 as well (which directs him with concrete tasks for the case).

– Meetings between LATHAM and source have been controlled by us.

– Information presented by source "LEON" are confirmed. It is true that LATHAM manifests interest in the .R.S.R. history and in particular in the Romanian-Hungarian relations. LATHAM participated in the recent seminar of American studies in Budapest. He invited there several Romanian researchers, but no such travel was approved.

– Recently, LATHAM and MUNSHI translated "Miorița" and will organize an exhibition on this subject. They will use a set of photographs made by former PhD candidate LAWRENCE SALZMAN in Sibiu area. We do not know yet the true motives of the activity, but the Council of Culture did not approve (for the time being) the opening of the exhibition (with much glitter) in Sibiu, Sighetul Marmației, and Rădăuți.

The three places were suggested by LATHAM.

– Both LATHAM and MUNSHI requested *to take the PhD exam* in Romania. LATHAM received the approval, MUNSHI did not.

They did this to extend their stay in Romania until 1987. The two of them were supposed to leave their job here this summer.

– LATHAM is watched very carefully, both by means of the network and through other means.

– *It is highly possible that his behavior should conceal an extremely subtle activity.*

– *He is certainly a C.I.A. officer.*

A.N.C.S.S.A., *Informative* fund, file no. 1093922, vol. II, ff. 222-224.

Handwritten indication at the beginning of document: "B.1/L.V."

* The seal of the respective institution was applied.

** Resolution: "Bureau I. / Very interesting person. Possibly Bureau "D." may use him to solve certain tasks in cooperation with 0544. Bring me suggestions. / SIG, undecipherable".

*** Underlined here and in the rest of the document.

-34-

Communication by Bureau III within County Inspectorate Bihor of the Ministry of Internal Affairs, to 3rd Directorate within D.S.S., to forward a note regarding shadowing of diplomat Ernest Latham, made in Oradea, on April 2, 1986

Socialist Republic Romania*   Top Secret

County Inspectorate Bihor / Securitate / Serv. III   Ex. no. 1

No. 310/0010429/04.07.1986

To the Ministry of Internal Affairs
Department of State Security / 3rd Directorate – Serv. I
Bucharest

Find attached, for exploitation, the note no. 0016303 of 04.03.1986 regarding the shadowing on LATHAM ERNEST, U.S. diplomat, who was in our area of competence on 04.02.1986.

Chief of Securitate, major, SIG, OGĂȘANU DUMITRU**

Chief Serv. III, col., SIG, ARONESCU C-TIN

[Annex]

Ministry of Internal Affairs   Top Secret

County Inspectorate Bihor / Serv. "F"   Exemplar no. 1

No. 0016303 of 04.03.1986

To the County Inspectorate Bihor / Bureau III

Ref. your request no. 0010429, we are forwarding you:

THE NOTE REGARDING THE SHADOWING ON LATHAM ERNEST, U.S. DIPLOMAT, CONSPIRATORIAL NAME "LASCU", WHO TRAVELLED BY CAR, LICENSE PLATE CD-1345, ON 04.02.1986

Activity of target "LASCU"

At 10.40, the target was taken under surveillance on Cluj-Oradea highway, in the commune Săcădat, while he travelled in the car CD-1345, together with the driver and an American stage director. They went on at high speed and entered the city of Oradea along Calea Clujului, following Calea 1 Mai, the bridge "23 August", Magheru street, "Lenin" park, 1 Decembrie 1918 street, Libertăţii park, I. Vulcan street, Republicii square, Victoriei square, Independenţei street, up to hotel "Vulturul Negru", where they stopped, after which, at the target's indication, the driver drove back to Victoriei square, parking next to the day bar.

The director and the target stepped down and entered "Vulturul Negru" passage up to the "Consignment" shop-windows, looking inside, then entered. They looked at the exhibits, walking separately to different places, then approached each other again, discussed something and the director went outside. The target looked carefully at the exhibits, then asked for a wall fabric (*peretar*), which he also examined and acquired for the amount of lei 800.

Meanwhile, the director went outside, went to a public weighting machine next to "Consignment", which he closely examined (there was no sign on it), climbed on it, quickly descended, took a paper out of his pocket, wrote down something (on the machine there was a list of ideal weighs, according to height, from the factory), then *he went to public WC****, used it, returned to the "Consignment" shop-window, looked inside and then passed along the windows of several shops in the area, looking at the exhibits, and when the target paid for the wall fabric he approached him, had a short exchange and came out together, walking to the car.

The target left the bought objects for the driver to put in the trunk and, together with the director, went into the day bar, where the director bought a parcel of cakes and went out. *The target returned to the "Consignment", looked at the shop-windows and then went to the WC*, used it, then returned to the car, where the director was waiting for him. They both entered the car and left the city in the direction of Arad, driving with moderate speed up to the commune Avram Iancu, where they ceased being shadowed at the county line, previously notifying Bureau "F" Arad, at 12.20 hours.

The shadowing on the target evinced the fact that he was especially interested in the objects at "Consignment", where he came on purpose and spent a considerable amount of time, buying a carpet and a wall fabric.

Find attached a photo album and the film which was used.

Chief of Bureau, lt.-colonel, SIG, VLAIC VASILE

Draft B.I. / typed by A.A. / R.D. 267/04.03.1986

[Annex]

A.N.C.S.S.A., *Informative* fund, file no. 1093922, vol. II, ff. 345-347.

Handwritten indication at the beginning of document: "B.1".

* Emblem of the R.S.R.

** Seal of the respective institution.

*** Underlined here and in the rest of the document.

-35-

Note by Bureau III within County Inspectorate Cluj of the Ministry of Internal Affairs, to 3rd Directorate within D.S.S., regarding the outcomes of informative proceedings undertaken on Ernest Latham and Russell Vandenbroucke in Cluj-Napoca, on April 1 and 2, 1986; Vandenbroucke – R.S.R. needs subventions for food, emigration is extremely small, and the population's mood – unfavorable; Latham – "in the near future Romania will need hard currency to import agricultural products"; again he – "communists have many difficulties and oblige population to prostitute"

Ministry of Internal Affairs	Top Secret
County Inspectorate Cluj / Bureau III	Ex. no. 1
No. 311/T.O./0015149 of 04.11.1986	

To the Ministry of Internal Affairs

Department of State Security / 3rd Directorate

Bucharest

Following your Order no. 001014 of 03.31.1986, referring to the American diplomat ERNEST LATHAM and VANDENBROUCKE JAMES, director of Theatre in St. Louis – U.S.A., we report that, as a result of informative operations undertaken (informative network, shadowing, fixed and portable T.O. means, video, secret searches), we have come to the following results:

In the morning of April 1, CY, after their arrival in Cluj-Napoca, the two Americans were received at the National Theatre by MARIA CRISTIAN, president of the County Committee for Culture and Art, HOREA

BĂDESCU, instructor in this committee, CONSTANTIN CUBLEŞAN, director of the Theatre, RADU BĂDILĂ, literary secretary, VICTOR TUDOR POPA, stage director and MARIN AURELIAN, actor. For the start, a presentation of the history of the National Theatre in Cluj-Napoca was made, followed by a dialogue on the relations to authors of dramaturgy, position of Romanian dramas in the repertoire, the actors' and stage directors' working regime and the manner in which the shows are approved.

Then, the group witnessed the rehearsal of a ballet show, during which VANDENBROUCKE JAMES slept for about 30 minutes.

Between 13.00 and 15.00, accompanied by MARIA CRISTIAN, president of the County Committee for Culture and Art, and RADU BĂDILĂ, literary secretary of the National Theatre, as a translator, the two Americans were received at the Hungarian State Theatre by the director KOTO IOZSEF, actress PANEK ANA, musical secretary IVA BARNA and instructor ZSIGMOND ISTVAN. The discussion evolved around the same themes, the presentation of the Theatre being followed by a dialogue on working conditions and the shows performed.

In the evening, the diplomat ERNEST LATHAM and VANDENBROUCKE JAMES witnessed a show at the National Theatre, accompanied by director CONSTANTIN CUBLEŞAN, literary secretary RADU BĂDILĂ and instructor HOREA BĂDESCU.

Although the officials with whom he talked positively introduced the activity of the two institutions, the American citizen VANDENBROUCKE J. tendentiously interpreted certain aspects. Thus, in the evening, in his hotel room, he recorded his impressions on a mini cassette recorder, alleging that our country needed assistance for food, that the emigration percentage was extremely low and the population's mood was unfavorable and, due to this reason, did not work with all the conviction.

Concluding that that Romanians were making obvious sacrifices in order to survive, he understood that the population's chances of success in life were diminished and this was the cause for the low work productivity as well.

Regarding the repertoire of the theatre, he understood it was not competitive, therefore the National Theatre needed subsidies, nevertheless underlying that the Hungarian Theatre was more representative and more efficient. The major problem for the Hungarian Theatre repertoire was the censorship of Romanian authorities, which assigned the productions and therefore plays were staged in Romania in virtue of an obligation, not of a commercial necessity. In his opinion, decisions in this field were taken by the state, not taking into consideration the artistic aspect of shows.

It is likely that VANDENBROUCKE J. intends to use these impressions in order to publish articles in newspapers in the U.S.A. It is worth noting that in all dialogues VANDENBROUCKE J. had with the diplomat ERNEST LATHAM he never mentioned the activities in the two visited theatres, as would have been normal, but mostly referred to political issues.

As a matter of fact, VANDENBROUCKE J. had a number of exchanges with the diplomat ERNEST LATHAM, during which the latter made a rather unfavorable presentation of the situation in our country. Thus, the diplomat affirmed that the Romanian currency did not have value on the foreign market and as a consequence the Romanian Government wished to get as much hard currency as possible, without wanting to spend it, in its turn.

E. LATHAM alleged in the near future Romania will need hard currency to import agricultural products. For the time being, he said, the Romanian Government did not promote this idea, but the Americans will have to persuade it and, probably, this will be his personal task. (It is worth mentioning that the political counsellor SCOTT EDELMANN, during a conversation with the American lecturer DIANA JOHNSON, in Cluj-Napoca, tackled the issue of American export of agricultural products to Romania, who for the time being did not agree to this idea. See our report no. 00141614 of 01.29.1986.)

The American diplomat was of the opinion that, because of centralized planning, Romania was stopped from her normal development. As for the rights of the Hungarian minority, he said they were maintained also due to diplomatic pressures, while, at the same time, his opinion was that some people would like to conceal the national issue, while others wanted to emphasize it.

Besides the official visits, the American diplomat went twice, accompanied by his Romanian driver, to the "Consignment" shop, where he bought plates adorned with folk motifs. On April 1st, CY, in the afternoon, E. LATHAM walked alone in the city center, and entered the University Bookstore, where he leafed through books unusually long (40 minutes), without talking to anyone. In the end, he bought the volume "History of Architecture in Romania" and a cooking book, which afterwards, in the hotel room, he never opened again. After leaving the bookstore, he went to the other side of the city Central Square, entered a tobacconist's and bought a box of *Snagov* cigarettes. Then he returned to the hotel room and smoked *Kent* cigarettes, out of the box he had with him ever since arriving in Cluj-Napoca. On the same day, in the evening, at the Theatre, he lit a *Kent* cigarette, and smoked the same *Kent* cigarettes upon returning to his hotel room.

It is noteworthy that on May 28, 1985 as well, while being in Cluj-Napoca, during the opening of the American exhibition "American Theatre Today", the diplomat E. LATHAM visited the "Consignment" shop and entered the University Bookstore, buying several books.

Taking into consideration this circumstance, we will take steps in the future for improved monitoring, technical means included, of activities he will carry out in that bookstore, for the purpose of tracing possible electronic communication.

Out of the persons with whom the American diplomat was in contact, only RADU BĂDILĂ, literary secretary of the National Theatre was in a visit of documentation in the U.S. In the morning of their arrival from the airport, while the two Americans were having breakfast in "Continental" restaurant, LIVIU MAIOR, lecturer at the Faculty of History, former grantee in the U.S., entered the room, but was not in touch with them, he was looking for the chief of the restaurant.

On April 2, CY, the two American citizens left by car, driven by the Romanian driver, for Timişoara.

Find attached the copies of 5 T.O. notes, as well as 97 photocopies*, from the diplomat's datebook, found during the secret search. One may draw the conclusion that the diplomat takes notes referring to the provisioning of the population and plans the meetings with various persons or writes down their addresses.

Chief of Securitate, colonel, SIG, undecipherable**

Chief of Bureau, lt.-colonel, SIG, VULCAN FILITAS

Drafted by T.O./Dact.O.V./R.D.178/491/2ex.

[Annex]

Notes made by E. LATHAM, found during the secret search on 04.01.1986 (made in his datebook)

Translated from English

Difference HITLER + Cers

Fishing for butter, oil, lemons

BRIGITTE BARDOT + frontiers of the country

Waiting for bread, eggs, (frozen?) meat, bring my people chairs.

Cluj has Jews, Hungarians, Romanians, we have party members.

A Hungarian child wants ice-cream, sings the *Tricolor* (*o.n.* with reference to a political joke).

[Annex]

Ministry of Internal Affairs   Top Secret

County Inspectorate Cluj / Bureau "F"   Ex. no. 1

No. 0034309 of 04.02.1986

To the Ministry of Internal Affairs - 3rd Directorate

Bucharest

NOTE REGARDING THE RESUMING OF SHADOWING TARGET "LASCU", ON APRIL 1, 1986, FROM 9.00 TO 22.00

Activity of the target

At 9.30, target "LASCU" and the American stage director accompanying him came out of "Continental" hotel, where they are hosted, stopped in front of the entrance for about 5 minutes, talked and looked around, then entered again the hotel.

At 9.55, target "LASCU" and the American stage director, who will be assigned the conspiratorial name "LIVIU" in our notes, the driver and RADU BĂDILĂ (known by the information body) came out of "Continental" hotel and got into the passenger car CD-1345, parked on str. Napoca, in front of the hotel.

The four of them went in the car driven by the driver along str. Na-poca, Piața Libertății, str. Dr. Petru Groza, Piața Victoriei and parked on the side of the National Theatre. Target "LASCU", "LIVIU" and RADU BĂDILĂ (known by the information body), who is accompanying them, stepped down and entered the Theatre, through the artists' entrance, at 10.00, while the driver and the car left for the city center.

At 10.50, the passenger car CD-1345, driven by the driver, stopped in the lateral parking lot of the National Theatre. Target "LASCU" alone came out of the Theatre at 12.00, got into the car, who went along Piața Victoriei, str. Petru Groza, Piața Libertății, str. Gh. Doja, E. Zolla, stop-ping in front of the "Consignment" shop. Target "LASCU" and the driver visited the two "Consignment" shops and the target bought several handicraft plates, worked in folk style.

At 12.50 target "LASCU" and the driver, carrying the goods that had been bought, came out of the shop, got into the car and immediately left along str. E. Zolla, Piața Muzeului, str. Săvinești, Poștei, Gh. Doja, Piața Libertății, str. Dr. Petru Groza, Piața Victoriei, stopping again in the parking lot next to the artists' entrance to the National Theatre.

Here target "LASCU" was expected by "LIVIU", RADU BĂDILĂ, who accompanied them to the hotel, as well as MARIA CRISTIAN, from the Theatre, and all got into the car. They all left through Piața Vic-toriei, str. Dr. Petru Groza, Piața Libertății, str. Gh. Doja, str. G. Barițiu, Aleea Tineretului, stopping in front of the Hungarian Theatre. They all got down and entered the Hungarian Theatre courtyard, at 13.10. The driver immediately returned to the car.

At 14.55 target "LASCU" together with "LIVIU", RADU BĂDILĂ and MARIA CRISTIAN, accompanied by other two men, officials within the Hungarian Theatre, came out of the Theatre yard and stopped next to the car CD-1345. They talked for about 5 more minutes, very formally, then took their leave and split.

Target "LASCU" and "LIVIU" got into the car CD-1345, with the driver, and immediately left for Aleea Tineretului, str. G. Barițiu, Doja, Piața Libertății, str. 30 Decembrie, Moților, Petru Maior, Piața Păcii, str. Napoca and stopped in front of "Continental" hotel, at 15.03.

Target "LASCU" and "LIVIU" got off the car and immediately walked to str. Napoca, up to the front of the shop "Mercur", where they watched the persons cuing for meat products, while talking and smiling, and after two minutes left the place and entered "Continental" hotel.

At 16.30 target "LASCU" and the driver left the hotel, got into the car CD-1345, and went down str. Napoca, Piața Libertății, str. Doja, E. Zolla and again stopped in front of the "Consignment" shop. Target "LASCU" and the driver got off the car and entered the "Consignment" shop, and "LASCU" was again interested in clay pots – folk style, and bought 10-15 plates which were wrapped up by the shop assistant. After about 10 minutes, the two of them walked out, the driver carrying the parcel, and got into the car. Then immediately left along str. E. Zolla, Săvinești, Poștei, Doja, Piața Libertății, and stopped in front of the St. Michael church, target "LASCU" stepped down and the car left.

Target "LASCU" crossed the square and stopped in front of the "Anticariat" shop, he looked at the windows, then entered the shop, at 16.46. He looked into several books in Romanian, without buying any.

At 16.53, target "LASCU" came out of the shop, went to the Liberty Square, stopping several times and looking into the shop windows along the way, continued along University Street and stopped to look into the windows of the University Library, and after 3 minutes entered the shop. Target "LASCU" visited most of the stands, leafed through many books, in some he read for minutes on end, and finally he bought three books, among which a cook book.

At 17.40, target LASCU came out of the book shop, holding three books, crossed Liberty Square in a hurry, then walked along 30 December Street and entered the Tobacco shop at the apartment complex at no. 4. After 1 minute, he came out with a box of *Snagov* cigarettes in his hand and walked hurriedly along 30 December street to Liberty Square, where he stopped, looked into the window of the shop "Arta Populară" (Folk Art), then he kept walking up to "Continental" hotel, which he reached at 17.52, holding the books he had bought.

It must be mentioned that all along his walk, "LASCU" looked carefully around, trying to leave the impression he was interested in the buildings and shop windows.

At 18.52, target "LASCU" and "LIVIU" came out of the hotel, the target with a book in his hand. He immediately got into the car CD-1345, parked in front of the hotel, with the driver waiting for them. They immediately left for str. Napoca, Piața Libertății, str. Dr. Petru Groza, Piața Victoriei, and stopped in front of the National Theatre.

Target "LASCU" and "LIVIU" got out of the car, "LASCU" produced a sheet of paper and explained something to the driver, reading from the paper, then they left, the car returning to the hotel. Target left the book in the car.

"LASCU" and "LIVIU" immediately entered the National Theatre, where they were met by MARIN AURELIAN, then they were approached by HOREA BĂDESCU, domiciled in Cluj-Napoca, str. Gr. Alexandrescu no. 24, sc. 3, et. 1, ap. 47. They talked in the hallway until the first signal, afterwards the entire group went up to box no. 11. During the intermission, they all came down to the hall and talked, target "LASCU" smoked a *Snagov* cigarette, he offered one to "LIVIU" as well, but they did not like it, they put them out and each lit a *Kent*.

At the end of the intermission, they went back to the box, watching the show "Lady Chirița in the Province". After the end of the show, target "LASCU" and "LIVIU", accompanied by MARIN AURELIAN and HOREA BĂDESCU, came out of the Theatre, and stopped for a while for a conversation. They were approached by CUBLEȘAN, director of the National Theatre, talked for about 2 more minutes, then shook hands and left, at 21.10.

Target "LASCU" and "LIVIU" walked away through Victoria Square, str. Dr. Petru Groza, up to the front of the shop "Adolescentul", where they suddenly turned and walked up to the front of the C.E.C. Agency. Here they stopped and asked a young man for directions to the "Continental" hotel. They received the needed explanation, then they turned again and walked down in a hurry along str. Dr. Petru Groza, to Piața Libertății and stopped in front of the University Bookstore. They looked at the window showing Comrade N. Ceaușescu's works and discussed for 3-4 minutes, then went down str. Napoca, and at 21.25 they entered the "Continental" hotel, and went up to the room.

Until 22.00, when shadowing was suspended, target "LASCU" did not leave the hotel.

Shadowing continues.

Chief of Bureau "F", colonel, SIG, POP SILVIU

2ex./MJR V.G./pm.D.O. / No. R.D. 0010/00335 of 04.02.1986

[Annex]

Rendered from the English language   Top Secret

I.D.B.T. – Cluj   Ex. no. 1

No. 0010687 of 04.02.1986   Serv. III

Lt. Col. TINCA O.

"HORIA" / *Duplicate*

[SPECIAL OPERATION]

A1 - ERNEST LATHAM

A2 - RUSSEL VANDENBROUCKE

18.30. A1+A2: A2 asks A1 the purpose of the consulate services. A1 answers that this is a section of the embassy granting visas and offering legal protection to U.S. citizens in a foreign country, even for penal cases.

He also speaks to A2 about the monetary exchange rate of the leu in relation to the U.S. currency. *"I wonder, - says A1, - how many times STEINBERG would have come to Romania to spend his money?" He says the leu does not have backing as a currency on the external market – it does not have gold backing. The Romanian Government wishes that foreigners should make as much currency exchange as possible, while Romania is not spending its hard currency.*

A1: They require us to pay our employees in the currency of the country. That is to say, we are paying our own dollars to the Romanian Government, and they transfer them in lei to the Romanian staff at the Embassy, do you understand? Who is handling the hard currency? The Romanian Government. We accommodate them. Do you get the point?***

A2: (Cannot be heard.) He is the same with the A2 at lunch.

A1: On the other hand, Romanians ask for hard currency for their products.

A2: (The same.)

A1: This brings them no benefit. They want hard currency (...)**** the communists have many difficulties and force the population to prostitute itself.

A2: (The same.)

A1: They will need hard currency to import agricultural products. For the time being, the Romanian Government did not put forth this idea. Probably we will have to convince them and probably this will be my task.

A2: (Cannot be heard.)

A1: Yes, in the sense of hard currency expenses. *We have a Cultural Agreement with the Romanian Government, which implies a number of exhibitions; the host country pays an amount – for packing and unpacking of the exhibits – that is to say, it bears a few internal costs.*

A2: Hotel (...)*****

A1: I don't know, certain aspects. For instance, in the higher education they get a quota for the invitees they have.

A2: (Cannot be heard.)

A1: For many years there was no significant Romanian exhibition in the U.S. We had "American Theatre Today".

A2: Whose idea was it?

A1: The U.S.'s. It was a tour, in a number of countries. It was shown in Budapest, Belgrade, Athens and in other places.

A2: What was it?

A1: Photographs, posters, videocassette recorders. The impact of the event was tremendous.

A2 asks to what degree was the population interested. *A1 says the interest was very high. Tickets could hardly be found. Queues formed up in the morning and lasted all day long. A fruitful experience for those who saw the exhibition and a lot of them – hundreds of Romanians – did not have a chance to actually enter the show hall itself.*

A1 keeps talking about the exhibition, in terms of shows (which he appreciates), explaining the exhibition was present in Bucharest in September, 1984 and in Cluj in July, 1985. The basic theme was one and the same. Only the actors and plays were different.

They each order a cup of coffee.

A1 says the hotel levies a 10% gratuity and that in Romania there is exclusively state property, none private. Everything is controlled and centralized, same as in the U.S.S.R.

A1: I want to give you a few examples, even contradictory, in order for you to better understand your own Romanian experience.

A2: And are frontiers open?

A1: In the sense that one may enter the country, yes. But there are a few transit points which are compulsory when crossing the frontier. Yugoslavia is preferred.

A1: It looks like the most impressive development in the '80 is Hungary's. The Yugoslavs are in stagnation, but Hungary pulls hard.

He also understands Hungarian and was in Budapest. He says Hungarians make a lot of fun of the Romanians, and their jokes refer to the Act of August 23 as well. He points out that, following the war, Hungary, Yugoslavia, Bulgaria, Romania, Albania, and Greece suffered under the impact of the conflict. He says Albania is at the 17th century level from the point of individual intellectual level. He says that Romanians are barred from their normal development by their own 5-year plans.

A2: I was hearing there are similarities between the two countries.

A1: We should not go that far. There isn't really a common level of comparison.

Then they speak about Cuba and the U.S., there are rockets in both places. The catastrophe is that the Cuban Revolution is in danger of spreading, due to Soviet policy of exporting revolution.

04.01.1986 / 18.54 hours/ 04.02.1986 / 14.34 hours

Drafted by lt.-maj. F.I.

R.D.142/354/Dactil.C.I./2ex.

[Annex]

Top Secret

Rendered from English

I.C.H. – Cluj   Serv. III

No. 0010687 of 04.02.1986   Lt. Col. TINCA

"HORIA" / *Copy*

[SPECIAL OPERATION]

A1 - ERNEST LATHAM,

Cultural attaché of the U.S. of A. in Bucharest

A2 - JAMES VANDENBROUCKE,

Director of the Theatre in St. Louis, U.S.A.

22.20. A2 in the room – I think he is recording on tape or writing:

1. Business hours (he mentions dinner and the fact restaurants in Cluj shut down at 21.00 and a visit to the Library).

2. Romania is a half-industrialized, half-agricultural country, which needs subsidies for food, especially from the U.S.

3. The percentage of emigrations from Romania is extremely low.

4. The mood of the population is also unfavorable; one hears the adage: "They pretend to pay us, we pretend to work for them".

5. Both Romanian men and women are, by nature, very unambitious, waiting for their own situation to be improved from the outside. Maybe the social-politic regime caused this attitude.

6. The chances of fulfilment in life of the population are diminished; they perceive this fact and, as a reaction, provide low productivity in their socialist labor.

7. Individual sacrifices in order to survive are obvious, for the reasons already mentioned.

8. The theatre repertoire is not competitive, the institution has to rely on subsidies in order to survive.

9. The Hungarian Theatre is more representative than the one in Romanian; the cultural expression is conceived differently and therefore efficient.

10. *The Romanian-American cultural agreement was not fulfilled according to expectations.* Nevertheless there are some hopes for the future, if an agreement is reached concerning the repertoire and principles of cultural exchanges.

11. Meeting with Dr. GÂLEA (?) He noted the prejudiced ideas that this woman has on culture.

12. A national cultural trend in Cluj; representative C. CUBLEŞAN, director of the National Theatre; he (CUBLEŞAN) knows from the very beginning that the repertoire options are not profitable. The National Theatre has in its repertoire 25/26 plays, out of which 6-7 are Romanian and the rest by foreign authors; 25 actors; 2 directors; 1 scenographer; 2 stage directors, technicians, etc. Out of the 25-26 shows, about 6 to 8 are for 10-12 year old children; about 8 plays are premiered every year. A scenographer's yearly norm is 4 productions. They tour the country, same as other Romanian theatres. About 100 shows per year; 3,000 spectators (!).

13. About 7-10,000 inhabitants of Hungarian origin in Cluj, who also speak Romanian.

14. Even the best shows of the Theatre did not have a public.

15. The way they are staged (technically) + show: they have no time to give it consideration, there are not sufficient rehearsals.

16. Salaries come from revenues, minus theater expenditures.

Conclusion: the National Theatre in Cluj is not competitive.

The history of the Theatre in Cluj was also approached in the dialogue with C. CUBLEŞAN. The hosts very graciously received the guests. A2 also witnessed a rehearsal of a new show, which he liked and considered it had commercial value.

17. At lunch, they met Professor RADU BĂDILĂ (?), who is also a critic and has a solid professional position both in Cluj and Bucharest.

18. In the afternoon, they visited the Hungarian Theatre; who they met (director's name?); 22 annual productions; 36 actors; the major problem in their repertoire is the censorship of Romanian authorities; productions are forced on them; with good actors, but who, in order to distinguish themselves, have to wait for the older actors' retirement. He mentions an actress who distinguished herself in the last two seasons; Hungarians are more active: they operate on the principle of demand and supply and stage what is required by the public. (*n.n.* se contradiction with above)******; the way the theatre is organized. The theatre director has the final word in choosing the repertoire.

CHIRIŢA: the character reflects a particular cultural level (having studied under somebody who did not know himself what he was teaching). He recounts the play; mentions the corruption evinced by the text and the extremely exaggerated features of the main character.

19. Productions staged in Romania are felt like an obligation, not as a commercial necessity, as in the U.S. (obligation-drudgery). Controversial subjects are avoided, in order to eliminate the "artistic pains of consciousness".

Decisions are taken by the state, which implicitly avoids the artistic aspect. In general, theater is traditionally oriented. Hence, a light production, full of comedy.

04.02.1986

Drafted by lt.-maj. F.I.

R.D.142/353/Dactil.C.I./2ex.

[Annex]

Ministry of Internal Affairs   Top Secret

County Inspectorate Cluj / Bureau "F"   Ex. no. 1

No. 0034309 of 04.03.1986

To the Ministry of Internal Affairs - 3rd Directorate

Bucharest

NOTE ON RESUMING THE SHADOWING ON TARGET "LASCU", ON APRIL 2, 1986, FROM 6.00 TO 09.00 A.M.

Target's activity

At 07.40 a.m. the driver came out of the hotel carrying a little suitcase, which he put into the trunk of the car CD-1345, parked in front of the hotel, then went back in. He returned to the car at 08.00, wiped the windows and prepared the car for the journey, then climbed in and waited.

At 08.42, target "LASCU" came out of the hotel, carrying a suitcase and a plastic bag, accompanied by "LIVIU", also carrying some luggage, and stopped next to the car. The driver stepped down and loaded the luggage into the trunk, while the two took their seats. Target "LASCU" explained something to the driver, indicating Liberty Square, then the three of them left by car along str. Napoca, Piața Libertății (Liberty Square), turned around at the church and stopped in front of the "Anticariat".

Target "LASCU" and "LIVIU" stepped out of the car and entered the church of St. Michael, at 08.49. The two of them looked at the interior of the church for 3 minutes, then came back to the car and immediately left through Liberty Square, via str. 30 Decembrie, Moților, Calea Mănăștur, Florești, Florești commune, where they reduced speed while passing in front of the military bases. After leaving the commune, at 09.00, they were left out of shadowing, upon order.

Conclusions:

During the two days of shadowing, outside of the official functions, target "LASCU" moved around through the city, alone or accompanied by the driver, visited twice the "Consignment" shop, where he purchased different objects, the "Anticariat", and the University Bookstore, buying books.

In the "Consignment" and the University Bookstore, target "LASCU" stood alone and for a very long time, examining the merchandise or leafing through various books.

It has been noticed that the target is very alert, controls discreetly and covers it by means of different proceedings (stopping abruptly and repeatedly, turning, stopping in front of shop windows).

We also mention that, during the entire period, the driver of the car CD-1345 watched very attentively the persons approaching the target.

The shadowing is over.

Chief of Bureau "F", colonel, SIG, POP SILVIU

2ex./MJR V.G./pm.D.O./No.R.D.0010/00337 of 04.03.1986

A.N.C.S.S.A., *Informative* fund, file no. 1093922, vol. II, ff. 226-228, 348-350; vol. V, ff. 13-16.

Handwritten indication at the beginning of document: "B.1/L.V./S.1".

* They were separately transmitted by the County Inspectorate Timiş to the 3rd Directorate of D.S.S., with the address no. 3/T.G./0063383 of April 05, 1986.

** Seal of the respective institution.

*** Underlined here and in the rest of the document.

**** Text interrupted in the document.

***** Text interrupted in the document.

****** Notes in the document.

Note by informer "OPREA" given to resident "CĂTĂLIN" on April 07, 1986 confirms the aspects resulting from the shadowing of ERNEST LATHAM carried out in Cluj (same file, vol. II, ff. 338-339).

-36-

Note by Bureau Relations V within the Ministry of Foreign Affairs regarding the conversation of Romanian diplomat Ilie Puşcaş with the American diplomats Ernest Latham and Henry Clark on the photo exhibition "Mioriţa", organized by the Press and Culture Section of the U.S. Embassy in Bucharest

Ministry of Foreign Affairs

Bureau Relations V   No. 5/1055

Comrade MARIA GROZA

Adjunct of the Minister

NOTE OF CONVERSATION

On April 29, 1986, on the occasion of a protocol event organized at the U.S. Embassy, HENRY CLARK, minister counsellor, and ERNEST LATHAM, cultural attaché at the U.S. Embassy, told ILIE PUȘCAȘ, secretary III at the Bureau Relations V, the following:

1) The Embassy highly appreciates the support received from the Council of Culture and Socialist Education to organize at the American Library the photograph exhibition "Miorița", which enjoyed an outstanding success.

2) The exhibition will also be opened at Brukenthal Museum in Sibiu, as well as in other places, to be established in mutual agreement with the leadership of C.C.E.S.

Taking into consideration that in the first part of May the exhibition is to be opened in Sibiu, the U.S. Embassy has kindly requested C.C.E.S. to approve the presentation of the exhibition for 3 days in the commune Poiana Sibiului, the place where the author took many of the photographs.

The period chosen for Poiana Sibiului is May 4 to 6, CY, which also coincides with one of the cultural events specific to the commune.

As the Embassy has not yet received the answer from C.C.E.S. and there is little time left until the opening of the exhibition, it solicits the support of the Ministry of Foreign Affairs to expedite the answer of the Council of Culture and Socialist Education.

SIG, undecipherable

April 30, 1986

Drafted by I. PUȘCAȘ / Dact. S. ANASTASIEI/2ex.

Ex.1-Comrade MARIA GROZA / Ex.2-DR.V

A.N.C.S.S.A., *Informative* fund, file no. 1093922, vol. II, ff. 352-353.

Handwritten indication at the beginning of the document:

1) "B.1/L.V."; 2) "S.I/526".

Registered: Office of Adj. of the Minster M.G. with

no. 152/04.30.1986-09.20-04.30.-10.30

Resolution: "Dr. V. / Please get in touch with C.C.E.S. and inform me. / SIG".

-37-

Bulletin of D.S.S. regarding the "Voice of America" broadcasting of Gabriela Lăzărescu's report on the exhibition "Miorița *Ballad* and the Confluence of Arts", organized in Bucharest by Ernest Latham and Melanie Munshi

MB 0544/282   For internal use

06.15.1986   Copy no. 3

RADIO BULLETIN NO. 182

The radio station "Voice of America" broadcasted a report read by GABRIELA LĂZĂRESCU *on the exhibition " Miorița Ballad and the Confluence of Arts", a Romanian-American cultural event recently opened at the American Library in Bucharest**:

"The American Library in Bucharest recently hosted the opening of an exhibition of a particular sort, the fruit of cooperation among arts. Present for this meeting were poetry, the art of image of the American photographer LAWRENCE SALZMAN, evoking scenes of the traditional pastoral life of Carpathian shepherds, as well as, thanks to the benevolence of the Village Museum in Romania's capital, traditional folk art objects lent to serve as a scenery to this event. The discreet background pastoral music, recorded on tape, contribute – in the white stylish halls of the American Library – to the atmosphere of an event unique in its own way – the *Miorița* exhibition.

As useful as they may be for laymen, the historical and literary explanations regarding the ballad *Miorița* are redundant for most of our listeners. *Relevant and remarkable is the interest manifested by the organizers of this exhibition – the American diplomats MELANIE S. MUNSHI, director of the American Library in Bucharest and ERNEST LATHAM – towards the twofold value of this meeting.* On the one hand, there is the confluence and dialogue of several arts – poetry, music, the art of translation – and, specifically, the art of merging LAWRENCE SALZMAN's images, employed here as a visual background to the ancestral and nevertheless eternally young message of the *Miorița*. On the other hand, and very significant, there is a Romanian-American dialogue harboring multiple valences which enrich the cultural dimension of mutual recognition.

The photographic images represent memorably plastic echoes of a journey undertaken by SALZMAN in the area around Poiana Sibiului, in the year 1981. They show expressive shepherds' portraits, old and young, glimpses from the life of mountain villages, moments from the folk ceremonials, moments of composure in front of the mystery of life and death. Of a most delicate evocative power are the American artist's photographs showing women and children in church and piously holding in their hands lit candles or carrying, according to custom, a ritual cross through the immaculate snow of the lane, in a hibernal village landscape. The lines of the ballad, vigorously translated by the two American diplomats, serve as a literary comment to the images, creating a succession of sublime rhymes, delicate connections between the deep meanings of

a Romanian folk text and the visual intuition of the American image artist.

*The Romanian-American event at the American Library in Bucha-
rest, devoted to the blending of meanings, tones and images raised by*
Miorița*, doubtlessly confirm the modernity of the ballad's theme".*

A.N.C.S.S.A., *Informative* fund, file no. 1093922, vol. II, ff. 371-372.

Handwritten indication at the beginning of the document:

1) "Dir. a III-a"; 2) "B.1".

* Underlined here and in the rest of the document.

-38-

Transcript of a phone conversation between Ernest Latham and the pastor of the Anglican
Church regarding the latter's replacement by
the diplomat during his absence from the R.S.R.

07.01.1986

Top Secret

Unique copy

MB 0625/311

"SILVIA" / 15.34 / called

The British pastor asks LATHAM whether he can "read" at the Anglican Church during the current month. L. says he will be in Bucharest
for the following two week-ends, therefore it will be ok.

The pastor informs him that on August 24 and 31, he will be in Bulgaria, then expresses his wish to see L. in order to speak to him. They decide to meet today at 17.00-17.15.

07.01.1986

SIG, undecipherable

A.N.C.S.S.A., *Informative* fund, file no. 1093922, vol. V, p. 127.

Handwritten indication at the beginning of the document: "B.1/H.C.".

-39-

Note by MB 0672/Bucharest, to the 3rd Directorate within D.S.S., regarding a meeting of the diplomat Ernest Latham with Caius Dragomir at "Continental" restaurant in Bucharest

Ministry of Internal Affairs	Top Secret
Department of State Security	Unique copy
MB 0672 – Bucharest	
No. D/00477132 of 07.19.1986	

To MB 0625/311

NOTE

On 07.10.1986, between 12.00 and 14.00 hours, target "LASCU" (LATHAM ERNEST), cultural attaché at the U.S. Embassy and CAIUS DRAGOMIR, in surveillance by MB 0625/3/2l, were at a table in "Continental" restaurant. They were served food and drinks and talked amicably.

The information authority was notified, and specific proceedings were undertaken.

Deputy commander of the Base, col., SIG, undecipherable*

Chief of Bureau, col., SIG, undecipherable

A.N.C.S.S.A., *Informative* fund, file no. 1093922, vol. III, p. 31.

Handwritten indication at the beginning of document: "B.1/H.C.".

* Seal of the respective military base.

-40-

Communication by MB 0544 to the 3rd Directorate within D.S.S., for forwarding of a note regarding allegations made by diplomat Ernest Latham on Romanian-American cultural relations; Latham on the inability of certain Romanian institutions to organize bilateral cultural activities

Ministry of Internal Affairs	Top Secret
Department of State Security	Copy no. 1
MB 0544	

No. 503/L/16/0030525 din 10.02.1986

To MB 0625 – Bucharest

Find attached, to be exploited, a note regarding certain comments made by the cultural attaché of the United States of America in Bucharest, ERNEST LATHAM, on the cultural relations between R.S. Romania and the United States.

Commander of Base, col., SIG, undecipherable

[Annex]

Top Secret

Copy no.*

NOTE

We are in possession of data from which it results that, related to the circumstances in which an agreement on the tour in our country by the American piano player of Armenian origins ARMEN DONELIAN was finally reached, the cultural attaché of the Unites States of America in Bucharest, ERNEST LATHAM, alleged that this success demonstrates that *certain restraints by the Romanian authorities to bringing to Romania messengers of American arts and culture are not dictated and accounted for by "political considerations"***, but by the organizational inability of Romanian specialized institutions.

Within the same context, ERNEST LATHAM pointed out that he was displeased – and will inform the American Government of this fact – with the difficulties faced by American intellectuals to contact personalities of Romanian culture, due to the approvals *the latter have to receive from the bodies of the Ministry of Internal Affairs and the Council of Culture and Socialist Education.* At the same time, he pointed out that A.R.I.A. is an institution with which it is impossible to cooperate properly, because of its staff members, who are careless, indolent, and disinterested in carrying out their professional responsibilities.

At the reception offered on September 25, 1986, at his domicile by the counsellor of the U.S. Embassy FRANK STROVAS, ERNEST LATHAM expressed, through gestures and words full of allusions, his certitude that conversations in his residence are being intercepted, clearly referring to this issue at a certain point, and using the term "monotorized" (sic.). As a matter of fact, when talking in the office of the director of the American Library in Bucharest, ERNEST LATHAM *habitually leads his interlocutor close to a ventilator heater, which functions continuously and produces a permanent and quite intense noise****.

A.N.C.S.S.A., *Informative* fund, file no. 1093922, vol. III, ff. 83-84.

* Rubric left blank.

** Underlined here and in the rest of the document.

*** Underlying accompanied by handwritten indication:

"Excerpt for synthesis *Issue of sec.*"

Resolution: "10.06.1986 / Bureau F. / What do we know? / SIG, undecipherable".

-41-

Note by D.S.S., based on the account made by informer "Joni", regarding his participation in a reception offered by Ernest Latham in honor of the pianist Armen Donelian and his conversation with the American diplomat; Latham – Romanian-American cultural exchanges at their lowest level, difficulties in bringing American specialists to the R.S.R.; the informer – "pleasant, jovial and has a sense of humor"

361/M.A.	Top Secret
Inf. "JONI"	Unique copy
House "Continental"	10.06.1986
File: 4561 / Register: 32	

NOTE

During the meeting on 10.06.1986, informer "JONI" reported the following:

On the occasion of the American pianist DONELIAN's visit to our country, the diplomat ERNEST LATHAM, cultural attaché at the U.S. Embassy, organized at his residence a dinner in the evening of 10.02. CY, to which were invited: KIKI MUNSHI, *MIHAI BERINDEI** and wife, actor *ION CARAMITRU, MIHAI HRISTU*, DONELIAN, and KIKI MUNSHI's Romanian secretary.

The informer reported that LATHAM complained that, *despite the efforts of the Cultural Section of the American Embassy, the cultural exchanges with our country have reached their lowest level this year, following the fact that Romanians were not allowed to make use of the grants offered by the Americans.*

Moreover, the Section has faced difficulties in bringing to our country American specialists to hold conferences at the American Library or Romanian institutions.

LATHAM told the informer that things went very well at the Council of Culture as long as the former referent ION MONAFU was in charge of relations with the U.S.A.

LATHAM also maintained that *because of the decree on protecting state secrets, Romanians no longer accepted the invitations made by* diplomats, giving various reasons.

KIKI MUNSHI scolded "JONI" for throwing a negative light on her versus other American diplomats, by his assertion that the Library's activity is far from what it was during CHAPLIN's or GREISS's time, and tried to convince him that circumstances had changed, in the sense that Romanians no longer respond to the invitations. KIKI MUNSHI drank quite a lot and got so tipsy that the situation became embarrassing at a certain moment. *ION CARAMITRU talked to BERINDEI, but also to LATHAM and KIKI MUNSHI.*

No other important aspects resulted.

On 10.02.1986, the source gave a jazz performance in which DONELIAN joined. After the concert, LATHAM congratulated "JONI" and told him he was content with the success DONELIAN registered and assessed that in the future the most efficient step for them to take was to bring to Romania cultural and artistic personalities who already are in Europe and who may organize events together with Romanians, and thus recoup part of their travel expenses, as DONELIAN gained a couple of thousands lei in just a few concerts. "JONI" made friends with LAT-HAM, as the informer is a pleasant, jovial man with a sense of humor. LATHAM told him he wished they might meet again, intending to offer "JONI" a 45 day grant and thought of preparing for him a program to include visits to all U.S. cities traditional for jazz, especially New Orleans and New York.

They agreed for "JONI" to go to the Library next week, in order to start rehearsals for a show to be organized there on the occasion of the presentation of a gala of the American Western movie, together with a conference given by IORDAN CHIMET, writer, author of a book on this subject a few years ago.

No other important aspects resulted.

N.O.

The informer was instructed and given the concrete mission regarding the necessity to cultivate relations with LATHAM and KIKI MUN-SHI, for the purpose of learning their official and unofficial activities, their comments, their circle of relations, the Romanians they come into contact with.

Lt. Col., SIG, undecipherable

A.N.C.S.S.A., *Informative* fund, file no. 1093922, vol. III, ff. 103-104.

*Underlined here and in the rest of the document.

Resolution: "Corroborate the data with the ones obtained by our network.

Exploit also in the checking materials. / SIG, undecipherable".

-42-

Phone conversation between Olga Maniu, employee of the U.S. Embassy in Bucharest, and Adrian Năstase, regarding his invitation by Ernest Latham

10.30.1986

Top Secret

Unique copy

MB 0625/311

"SILVIA" / 10.13 a.m. / Calls 151198

OLGA MANIU tells ADRIAN NĂSTASE that an invitation has been sent to him at A.D.I.R.I., for November 7, at LATHAM's.

A.N. says he has not picked it up yet and will take the necessary steps. He asks the Embassy to kindly send him the invitations to the Institute. He will provide the answer to the invitations later.

10.30.1986

Rendered by CPT P.M.

A.N.C.S.S.A., *Informative* fund, file no. 1093922, vol. V, p. 182.

Handwritten indication: 1) "B.1/A.I."; 2) ADRIAN NĂSTASE is under the scrutiny of MB 0544. / Lt.-maj., SIG, undecipherable".

-43-

Note by informer "Florina" regarding her participation in a conference organized by the Press and Culture Section of the U.S. Embassy in Bucharest and her conversation with Ernest H. Latham; Silviu Brucan "talked for a long time" with Latham and Melanie Munshi

351/S.T.   Top Secret

"FLORINA"   Unique copy

No. 66137/00242/12 Dec. 1986

NOTE

On December 8, CY, I was invited to the American Library for a conference on the Constitution of the United States. Since the speaker did not arrive, because of an airplane failure, I only took part in the cocktail that was supposed to follow the conference. A number of persons unknown to me were present, probably jurists and specialized researchers.

Among the ones I know, the following participated: TUDOR POPESCU, researcher at "Ştefan Gheorghiu", with his wife, a sociologist; the literary critic GHEORGHE MUNTEAN with his wife; the former ambassador SILVIU BRUCAN; OLGA MANIU, a clerk at the U.S. Embassy; Mrs. GOGA, translator at the American Library; ANCA GIURESCU, university professor; professor DAN GRIGORESCU and his wife; representatives of the Council of Culture and Publishing Houses Central; professor AL. DUŢU.

The participating foreigners were only the director of the Library, KIKI MUNSHI, cultural counsellor ERNEST LATHAM, and SEDLEY, from the Commercial Section.

As soon as I arrived, both the Library director and ERNEST LAT-HAM approached me and asked about my impressions upon returning from the U.S. and to enquire about the details of the program organized for me.

They were the first American diplomats with whom I talked after my return.

As there were so many Romanians and few foreigners, the Romanians were naturally talking among themselves. The former ambassador SILVIU BRUCAN talked at length with ERNEST LATHAM and KIKI MUNSHI. TUDOR POPESCU was also talking a lot to the foreign diplomats, as usual.

N.O.

"FLORINA" gave the present Note following our instructions regarding the participation in receptions.

A copy of the note will be forwarded for further use at Serv. 1.

As on December 20, CY, she will participate in a dinner offered at the U.S. Library, new tasks will be given to her, in mutual agreement with the line bureau.

Colonel SAVA TOMIȚĂ

R.D.1884/B.N./unique copy

A.N.C.S.S.A., *Informative* fund, file no. 1093922, vol. III, p. 165.

Handwritten indication: 1) "S.1"; 2) "LASCU";

3) "BLANSTEIN ALBERT PAUL".

-44-

Note by informer "Lovinescu" regarding the preface made by diplomat Ernest Latham to the translation of the "History of Romanian Literature", by George Călinescu

Source: "LOVINESCU"

Domicile   02.25.1987

02.26.1987 / No. 00190

INFORMATIVE NOTE

On 02.21., TRAIAN FILIP's son, arrived from Italy, brought to me 50 pages from the "History of Literature", by G. CĂLINESCU, English text, paginated, as well as prof. DRĂGAN's preface (translated by me), and the one and a half page long "preface" (in English) by the U.S. cultural attaché, ERNEST LATHAM.

It is not actually a "preface", but a short viewpoint, which I finally entitled in English "A foreigner's point of view". Taking into consideration the background, according to Mr. LATHAM's letter: "neither my position of a cultural attaché, nor my place of work, the American Embassy, can be made public in the context of this preface, as the regulations governing the American Foreign Accreditation Service prohibits specifically mentioning any such references in a work such as the *History of the Romanian Literature*, by G. CĂLINESCU", I considered it was better to preserve the signature under the form, "ERNEST H. LATHAM, JR., Bucharest, Romania, February 4, 1987", without any other specification.

Personally, I consider this "preface" to be correct, although I do not totally agree with the idea that "the first edition was never reprinted in

Romania" (the 1982 edition was "revised and enlarged", claims Mr. LATHAM, but prof. PIRU, its editorial supervisor, claims it is faithful to the 1941 edition, with unimportant corrections, concerning data revised by the author himself, while prof. DRĂGAN, in his own preface, speaks of "regrettable omissions/reductions"). I cannot take a firm position, because I have not collated the two texts; as a translator of the 1941 text, I wondered what could have been omitted (as "regrettable")?

On 02.24. TRAIAN FILIP paid me a short visit bringing me 100 more pages for the final proof reading and we talked about the perspectives to print the work. I still have to proofread another approximately 700 pages, which he will bring in 2-3 weeks, when he returns (his wife is seriously ill). In Milan, the printing process advances with very much difficulty (the typist is overloaded, there always show up more urgent tasks, for example a brochure-response to G. RĂDULESCU's "anti-Thracian" article published in "România Literară", the Italians obstruct in every conceivable manner, replace the printing house cassettes, destroy materials, etc.).

TRAIAN FILIP assured me the book will certainly be published in May 1987. Let me mention he also left me a copy of a document showing U.N.E.S.C.O. is authorizing prof. DRĂGAN to publish the volume under U.N.E.S.C.O. aegis, with the note: "The present book has been prepared in the spirit of the Declaration of the Principles of International Cultural Cooperation adopted in 1966. It was inspired by the same ideals on which U.N.E.S.C.O.'s efforts for intercultural dialogue are based".

SIG, undecipherable

Note of the Bureau

The publication of the "History..." and "LOVINESCU"'s involvement are ongoing activities, and the source is to this end in contact with the cultural attaché of the Embassy in Rome, TRAIAN FILIP.

Taking into consideration "LOVINESCU" has been in no way in touch with British diplomats or any other British citizens (nor was he invited to receptions for the past 4 or 5 years), and his relations to LATHAM were limited to the latter's examination for the Ph.D., and the last talk, controlled by us through I.D.B.T. (exploited by Serv. I as well), took place in October 1986, and since then, he (LATHAM ERNEST, U.S. cultural attaché in Bucharest, "LOVINESCU"'s PhD candidate) never met him again, we will be in touch with Serv. 1 and Serv. 11 in the 3rd Directorate, in order to put him at their disposal, according to their needs.

Material is exploited at Bureau 1.

CPT, SIG, CĂLBĂJOS VASILE

[Annex]

Embassy of the United States of America*

Strada Tudor Arghezi 7-9

Bucharest, Romania

Press and Cultural Section

February 5, 1987

To Mr. Prof. Dr. IOSIF CONSTANTIN DRĂGAN

President

Drăgan Foundation

Str. Dr. Lister 6

Esteemed Mister Professor DRĂGAN,

Please receive the attached possible preface to the English language version of the "History of Romanian Literature" by GEORGE CĂLIN-ESCU. It may correspond to the manner in which you would want it to be conceived.

I have to underline that both my function of Cultural Attaché, and the place I work in, namely the American Embassy, cannot be made public in the context of this preface, as the regulations governing the American Foreign Accreditation Service prohibits specifically mentioning any such references in a work such as the "History or Romanian Literature", by GEORGE CĂLINESCU.

I trust this will not constitute in any way an impediment for you, in case you decide to publish the preface written by me.

Please receive my best wishes and I hope I will have the opportunity to see you again soon.

With high esteem,

SIG, ERNEST H. LATHAM JR.

Cultural Attaché

1 annex

[Annex]
PREFACE TO CĂLINESCU'S HISTORY OF ROMANIAN LITERATURE: FROM ITS ORIGINS TO THE PRESENT

When Dumitru Micu entitled his study *G. Călinescu: Between Apollo and Dionysos*, he was suggesting to his readers the complexity and extent of Călinescu's contributions to Romanian culture and literature. Although an accomplished novelist, poet, playwright, critic, and journalist, Călinescu's most enduring claim to attention will likely be the vast survey of Romanian literature now made accessible to the English-reading world for the first time, nearly half a century since it was first published.

This unconscionable lapse of time in part can be explained, albeit, not excused, by recalling that when this work was first published in 1941 the European continent was two years into the Second War. The politics and battle lines of the time had separated Romania from the English-speaking world, and national priorities in wartime accord little attention to literary history of whatever merit. Under these circumstances, it is hardly surprising that few copies of Călinescu's history made their way out of Eastern Europe. When peace returned to the world in 1945, it brought with it to Romania a new set of priorities and political realities into which apparently Călinescu's vision did not comfortably fit. A second, significantly "revised and enlarged" edition of Călinescu finally appeared in Romania in 1982, some seventeen years after the author's death. The first edition has never been reprinted in Romania.

Thus, the present translation is doubly to be welcomed, for not only does it offer to the English-reading world the fundamental survey of Romanian literature but also does so in the edition which the author himself saw through the press. Indeed, the translation is triply to be welcomed because it bears the name of Professor Leon Levitschi, a distinguished Romanian scholar of English letters, whose professional life has been devoted to translations, lexicography, and literary criticism between the two literatures and who brings to the present work skills and sensitivities sharpened over many years.

Mention also be made here of Iosif Constantin Drăgan and the Drăgan European Foundation without whose resources this considerable effort might well never have been undertaken. Dr. Drăgan has earned once again the gratitude of all who believe that Romanian culture and literature have an importance beyond the confines of the Balkans and deserve the widest possible exposure. With his generous support of this publishing effort, Dr. Drăgan has insured that a central element of this culture will for the first time be accessible in parts of the world where Romanian literature has been too little known or studied heretofore.

ERNEST H. LATHAM, Jr.

Bucharest, Romania

February 4, 1987

A.N.C.S.S.A., *Informative* fund, file no. 1093922, vol. III, ff. 195-198bis.

Illegible handwritten indication at the beginning of the document.

* The U.S. coat of arms.

-45-

Note regarding the visit of diplomats Ernest
Latham and Melanie Munshi to Galați, on March
25, 1987; two Romanian citizens' unauthorized,
"abusive" and "uncivilized" participation in
an American exhibition; the diplomats' preoccupation with the dissemination of the "Miorița" poster

[March 1987]

REPORT CONCERNING THE VISIT OF THE DELEGATION
OF THE U.S.A. EMBASSY IN BUCHAREST
TO GALAȚI MUNICIPALITY

On March 25, 1987, 16.00 hours, the headquarters of the County
Museum of History hosted the opening of the exhibition of art photographs made by WILL M. AGAR including children books published in
the U.S. The exhibition was traveled to Galați, through the Council of
Culture and Socialist Education, and the materials were brought to Galați
from Ploiești on March 23, CY, by Comrade AVRAM, employed by the
U.S. Embassy.

KIKI SKAGEN MUNSHI, director of the American Library in Bucharest and ERNEST LATHAM, JR., cultural attaché at the U.S. Embassy in Bucharest arrived at 15.55, on 03.25.1987, in the exhibition hall,
for the opening. The talks and protocol unfolded as follows:

– At 16.00 hours the exhibition was officially opened. Opening re-
marks were given by Comrade ION IORDACHE, vice-president of
C.J.C.E.S. and STANCIU ȘTEFAN, director of the Museum Complex
Galați, from the Romanian side, and ERNEST H. LATHAM Jr. from the
American side.

KIKI MUNSHI made a presentation of the books in the exhibition.

– At 16.30 hours, the American delegates offered a dinner, within the exhibition, in which there took part 25 persons proposed and approved by the Galați County Committee of Culture and Socialist Education. Although they were insistently cautioned to take their leave, STERIAN VICOL, journalist, and ANGELA TOMASELLI-HOLBAN, professor and artist, abusively took part in the event. I do not know the reason why they insisted on participating in an absolutely uncouth manner.

During the dinner, the conversations with U.S. representatives in which they took part were not personal, but only in a group, in Romanian, touching upon the following subjects:

– history of the town of Galați;

– cultural Romanian-American contacts;

– cultural ties between Dacians and Greeks in ancient times.

Among the other participants, the following carried out more direct dialogues with the American representatives:

– MARCU AURORA, CRIȘAN MARIA (with KIKI MUNSHI, I was not close enough to find out the subject), ITU NICOLAE, STERIAN VICOL, IORDACHE ION etc.

At the end of the dinner, the guests were thanked by Comrade VASILE BRUTAS, secretary of the Galați County Committee of P.C.R..

Between 18.00-18.45, together with Comrade ION IORDACHE and the American delegates, I went to the "V.A. Urechia" Library, where Comrades OPREA NEDELCU and PAUL PALTANEA presented rare books in the collection of the library, especially ones bearing important autographs. They showed their enthusiasm and interest in autographs of VASILE ALECSANDRI, MIHAIL KOGĂLNICEANU, and MARK TWAIN. As I had to take a phone call, I was not permanently close to the guests. The library director offered coffee, and the dialogue evolved around the organizing of libraries. NEDELCU OPREA, IORDACHE ION, and STANCIU ȘTEFAN represented the Romanian side.

Between 17.30-21.30 hours, I participated with the American delegates and Comrade IORDACHE ION in the show "Litoral-calor", presented by "Fantasio" Theatre from Constanța at the Trade Union Community Center. The delegates were welcomed by the director, POPOVICI ALEXANDRU. Before the show, Mrs. KIKI MUNSHI asked the director about the way the institution is self-financing. Other talks were trite (about California climate, aspects from India etc.).

At 21.45 I took my leave from the delegates, who went to the hotel, accompanied by Comrade ION IORDACHE.

The following day, March 26, 1987, at 09.20 hours, I met again the American delegates in front of "Galați" hotel, accompanied by museographer RÎPĂ DAN BUICLIU and we went on a visit to the feudal art monument "Precista".*

The presentation of the "Precista" exhibition was made by the museographer RÎPĂ DAN and the cultural counsellor of Dunărea de Jos Archbishopric, priest DRĂGOI. The talks only referred to the monument and the history of the city. Mr. LATHAM took pictures of the exterior of the monument.

At Mr. AVRAM's signal, the guests entered the "Consignația" shop in the area and bought 2 samovars, made in Russia before 1917.

From the bookshop and *anticariat* on str. Republicii, next to the Dramatic Theatre, they bought children's books in English (author JOSE MARTI), "Bibliografia Independenței" and "Franceza utilă pentru copii", by MARCEL SARAȘ.

---

*Fortified Church of the Holy Virgin in Galati.

I took my leave from the guests in front of the book shop around 12.00, and they left for Bucharest.

I want to draw the attention on their preoccupation with disseminating the "Miorița" poster (2 copies were left at "Precista" and more at the Museum of History), a poster which is not approved for public distribution.

2ex./L.O.

A.N.C.S.S.A., *Informative* fund, file no. 1093922, vol. III, ff. 225-226.

–46–

Note by Bureau III of the Galați County Inspectorate of the Ministry of Internal Affairs to the 3rd Directorate within D.S.S., regarding the participation of diplomats Ernest Latham and Melanie Munshi in the opening of an exhibition of photographs of Will Agar on March 25, 1987, in Galați; the visit with to the diplomats at their hotel by a Romanian citizen

Ministry of Internal Affairs	Top Secret
Galați County Inspectorate	Ex. no. 1
Securitate – Bureau 3	
No. 311/P.I./0023544/04.09.1987	

To M.I. – D.S.S. 3rd Directorate

Bucharest

On March 25, 1987, LATHAM ERNEST, cultural attaché of the U.S. Embassy and MUNSHI MELANIE-KIKI, director of the American

Library in Bucharest, were present in our range of activities to participate in the opening of the exhibition of photographs made by the photographer WILL AGAR, with reference to children's books published in the U.S.A., at the Section of History of the Galați County Museum Complex.

The intelligence proceedings undertaken (sources both capable and confirmed in action were deployed; shadowing; recording at appropriate moments with I.D.B.T. means; housing T.O.) resulted into the following events of operational interest:

MUNSHI MELANIE made a presentation of the books exhibited, then the American delegation offered a dinner for 25 participants as nominated and approved by the Galați County Committee of Culture and Socialist Education. The issues addressed during the conversations referred to the history of the town of Galați, Romanian-American cultural contacts, cultural ties between Dacians and Greeks in ancient times.

After dinner, they visited the library "V.A. Urechia", where they were shown rare exhibits, specially important autographs present in the collection. They expressed their enthusiasm and interest in the autographs of VASILE ALECSANDRI, MIHAIL KOGĂLNICEANU, and MARK TWAIN.

Afterwards, they attended a show at the Trade Union Community Center; MUNSHI MELANIE took advantage of this opportunity to ask the director about the way the institution is self-financing.

On March 26, CY, they visited the monument of feudal art "Precista".

During the visit, MUNSHI MELANIE was concerned with advertising the magazine "Sinteza" and the "Miorița" poster. Steps were taken to limit the distribution of these materials.

VICOL STERIAN, local journalist and "Agerpres" correspondent and TOMASELLI ANGELA, professor and artist* took part in the

Targeted as a Spy

dinner organized on March 25, without approval, despite the fact that they had been advised by the officials to leave.

VICOL STERIAN, born on May 9, 1943, in the commune Tuțcani, Vaslui county, son of DUMITRU and ILINCA, domiciled in Galați, str. Egalității, Bl. Lebăda, sc. 1, ap. 5, *unofficially visited the Americans at the hotel*, which demonstrates their interest to cultivate and make permanent their relationship with him. During discussions, the cultural attaché questioned him regarding the domains in which he collects information for the local newspaper "Viața Nouă" (New Life) and invited him to visit the Library during his trips to Bucharest.

Find attached the content of talks among VICOL STERIAN, the cultural attaché and the director of the American Library, 1 cassette; 1 T.D.K. cassette (c.1975-1977) including recordings of the dialogue between LATHAM ERNEST and MUNSHI MELANIE at "Galați" restaurant, we kindly ask for the cassette to be returned to us after playing it, 3 briefing notes and 2 "F" materials referring to their activity and behavior.

Chief of County Securitate, major, SIG, LUPU VIOREL**

Chief of Bureau 1, major, SIG, URSU NICOLAE

[Annex]

Ministry of Internal Affairs	Top Secret
Galați County Inspectorate / Securitate – Bureau "F"	Unique copy
No. 0027328 of 03.27.1987	

To Bureau III- Intern

No. 023445 of 03.25.1987

NOTE REGARDING THE SURVEILLANCE OF LATHAM ERNEST – "LIVIU", CULTURAL ATTACHÉ OF THE U.S. EMBASSY IN BUCHAREST, TEMPORARILY LODGED IN HOTEL "GALAȚI", ROOM...***, CARRIED OUT ON 03.25 AND 26, 1987

Way of identifying him

The target was recognized by taking into consideration his features and the license plate of the car CD-1345.

Target's activity

On 03.25.1987, surveillance started at 11.30 hours, at the town line of Galați Municipality.

At 14.25, target "LIVIU" accompanied by MUNSHI SKAGEN, director of the American Library in Bucharest and the car driver entered the area of responsibility, travelling in the car CD-1345 along Brăila-Galați highway and continuing along Șoseaua Șendreni-Galați, str. Brăilei, stopping in the parking lot in front of "Dunărea" hotel.

The three of them stepped down here – "LIVIU" was carrying a beige suitcase and entered "Dunărea" hotel, whence they came out in 5 minutes and, carrying the same hand luggage, crossed B-dul Republicii, and entered "Galați" hotel, at 14.45 hours.

At 15.10 "LIVIU" together with the director of the American Library came out of the hotel, crossed B-dul Republicii and walked along str. Brăilei, entering in the Central Bookstore, the department of school supplies, left immediately and entered the book department. The two of them perused several books for 20 minutes, then the target bought seven books of old history of Romania, the director three books, departed the bookstore with them, walking along str. Brăilei, then crossed B-dul Republicii, stopping in front of "Galați" hotel, at that moment when they were welcomed by a Romanian official, representing the Galați County Committee of Culture and Socialist Education with the drivers of the cars CD-1333 and CD-1345.

After exchanging greetings and talking for a few minutes, they left; the driver of the car CD-1333 left in this car along B-dul Republicii towards "Modern" shop, while "LIVIU" and the director left the books they had bought in the trunk of the car CD-1345, then boarded the car in the following manner: "LIVIU" in the back right seat, the director left, and the Romanian official in front, next to the car driver.

Hence they travelled along str. Brăilei, Stadionului, the highway next to the Water House, the Danube Waterfront, going down to the ferry crossing the Danube, travelling at low speed through the Park for Metal Sculpture up to the Captain of the Port offices, then along str. 13 Iunie, Waterfront, B-dul Republicii, 23 August, Al. I. Cuza, stopping in front of the Museum of History.

Here the four of them stepped down, and were greeted by the director of the Museum of History and another official, they exchanged greetings and entered the museum, followed by the driver of the car CD-1345, holding a travel refrigerator, at 15.55 hours.

At 17.50 hours, "LIVIU" came out of the Museum together with the director of the American Library – the director of the American Library was holding several bunches of flowers – the director of the Museum and the representative of the County Committee of Culture and Socialist Education and left in the car CD-1345 (driver was at the wheel), along str. Al. I. Cuza, Gării, M. Bravu, stopping in front of the Library "V.A. Urechia", where "LIVIU" and the other three stepped down and entered the library – the car driver stayed in the car – at 17.55 hours.

At 18.50, "LIVIU", the director of the American Library, the director of the Museum of History and the representative of the Committee of

Culture and Socialist Education came out of the Library "V.A. Urechia", boarded the car CD-1345 and went along str. M. Bravu, Gării, B-dul Republicii, str. Brăilei, B-dul G. Coşbuc, stopping in the parking lot in front of the Trade Union Community Center. "LIVIU" and the persons accompanying him, except the driver, stepped out of the car and entered the Trade Union Community Center, where the show of the Fantasio Theatre in Constanţa was to start, at 19.00 hours.

At 19.10 hours, the car CD-1333 also stopped in the parking lot in front of the Trade Union Community Center, from which stepped down the driver and another Romanian official from the U.S. Embassy in Bucharest and, together with the driver of the car CD-1345 entered the Trade Union Community Center.

The intelligence officer in charge was ordered to take over inside, where the surveillance was unable to penetrate.

At 21.30 hours, the driver of the car CD-1345 came out of the Trade Union Community Center, took his place in the car and waited.

At 21.45 hours, "LIVIU", the director of the American Library in Bucharest and the representative of the County Committee of Culture and Socialist Education came out of the Trade Union Community Center, boarded the car CD-1345 and went along B-dul G. Coşbuc, str. Brăilei, to stop in the parking lot in front of "Galaţi" hotel. Here they all stepped out of the car in front of the entrance to "Galaţi" hotel, the representative of the County Committee of Culture and Socialist Education took his leave, shaking hands with "LIVIU" and the director of the American Library, then they left; "LIVIU" and the director entered the hotel, at 22.00 hours, and the representative of the County Committee of Culture and Socialist Education took his leave from the driver of the car CD-1333 and the Romanian official from the U.S. Embassy in Bucharest (who meanwhile had arrived in the car CD-1333), then left along str.

Brăilei to str. Traian. The two car drivers locked their cars, then entered the hotel.

The shadowing continued until 22.00 hours, when it was interrupted, as ordered; while target "LIVIU" did not come out of the hotel again.

On 03.26.1987, surveillance started, as ordered, at 06.30 hours, at "Galați" hotel, where the target was located.

From 07.45 to 08.30, the driver of the car CD-1333, named DUMI-TRESCU ȘTEFAN, and the translator from the U.S. Embassy in Bucha-rest, named AVRAM VASILE, brought out of the hotel several pieces of luggage, which they put into CD-1333, then stayed at the car.

At 08.05 hours, the driver of CD-1345 came out of the hotel carrying two plastic bags, and put into the trunk of the car CD-1345, then stayed there, talking to AVRAM V. and DUMITRESCU Ș.

At 08.30 hours, AVRAM V. and DUMITRESCU Ș. left in CD-1333 for the Museum of History, on str. Al. I. Cuza, and entered the exhibition.

At 08.15 hours the driver of CD-1345 left by car for str. Brăilei and returned to the hotel at 08.35.

At 09.15 hours, CD-1333 returned in front of the hotel, bringing AVRAM, DUMITRESCU and two Romanian clerks, and the director of the Museum of History remained in front of the hotel, talking to the driver of CD-1345.

At 09.25 hours, target "LIVIU", carrying a little travel suitcase and a camera, came out of "Galați" hotel, together with the director of the American Library in Bucharest, who carried on her shoulder a small travel bag, and were met by the driver of CD-1345, who took their lug-gage and stored it in the trunk of the car CD-1345. Then, they were ap-proached by AVRAM, DUMITRESCU and the Romanian clerks, who exchanged greetings with the target, and talked for about 3 minutes in front of the hotel.

At 09.28 hours, target "LIVIU", the director of the American Library and the director of the Museum boarded CD-1345 (its driver at the wheel), and DUMITRESCU S., AVRAM V. and the other Romanian clerk boarded CD-1333. They all left (CD-1345 in front) along B-dul Republicii, Danube Waterfront, stopping close to the crossroads with str. Traian, where they all stepped down and entered "Precista" church, at 09.33 hours.

After approximately 15 minutes, the drivers of both cars came out of the church, came back to their cars, then walked to the "Consignația" store, they entered it, then returned to their cars.

At 10.15 hours, target "LIVIU", the director of the Library, the director of the Museum and the Romanian clerk came out of the church, accompanied by the priest and another individual, and stopped at the grave stones next to the church. The priest offered explanations to the group. After 2 minutes, the director of the American Library went to the car CD-1345, and returned to the group holding a color photo album, which she gave to the priest.

At 10.25 hours, target "LIVIU", the director of the American Library, the director of the Museum and the Romanian clerk took their leave from the priest and the fellow mentioned above (who both entered the church) and went to the cars, where the driver of CD-1345 said something to "LIVIU", pointing to the "Consignație". Target "LIVIU" and the group went along str. Traian, stopping approximately 30 meters in front of block P-11 (in the park, facing the church), and target "LIVIU" took several pictures of "Precista" church. Hence they went as a group to "Consignația", at the ground floor of block P-11. Meanwhile, the drivers parked the cars in front of "Consignația", at 10.30 hours.

After 10 minutes, AVRAM V. came out of the shop carrying a parcel wrapped in white paper, the size of a foreign beer box, which he deposited in the trunk of the car CD-1345, then he entered again the shop and came out again, after 10 minutes, holding a parcel wrapped in white paper, having the dimensions of a flower vase approximately 30 cm wide and 40 cm high, which he put into the trunk of the above mentioned car, then stayed at the car, taking to the two drivers.

Note: target "LIVIU" was not monitored inside "Consignația" shop, as conditions were not proper.

At 11.00 hours, target "LIVIU", the director of the American Library, the director of the Museum and the Romanian clerk came out of "Consignația" and approached the cars CD-1333 and CD-1345, kept talking for about 3 minutes, then boarded the cars: target "LIVIU", the director of the American Library, the director of the Museum in *CD-1333 and they all left along B-dul Republicii, and close to Str. Navelor slipped from surveillance* at 11.07 hours****.

At 11.20 hours, target "LIVIU", the director of the American Library and the driver were spotted coming in the car CD-1345 along B-dul Republicii from the shop "Modern", continuing along str. Brăilei, Șoseaua Galați-Brăila, and stopped at the gas station Șendreni. Here the driver filled his tank with gasoline, then the three of them left along the Galați-Brăila highway, and after they crossed the river Siret shadowing was stopped, according to the request, at 11.40 hours.

We note that at 12.00 hours, the car CD-1333, with AVRAM VASILE and DUMITRESCU ȘTEFAN on board, was seen crossing the river Siret to Brăila county, towards Brăila municipality.

During surveillance, target "LIVIU" behaved normally, was accompanied most of the time by the director of the American Library and the Romanian clerks, along with whom he visited some areas of the city and "Precista" church.

In the first day of surveillance, he participated in the opening of the American exhibition and watched a show at the Trade Union Community Center.

The driver of the car CD-1345 was deferential to the director of the American Library.

The photographs resulting from documenting these movements will be sent separately.

Surveillance was terminated.

Chief of Bureau "F", Lt. Col., ss, BLEOJU NECULAI

R.D./196/64/03.27.1987/Conc.23/40/Dac.20/unique copy.

[Annex]

Ministry of Internal Affairs	Top Secret
Galați County Inspectorate / Securitate – Bureau "F"	Unique copy
No. 0027352 of 03.30.1987	

To Bureau III - Intern

On 03.23.1987, 16.05 hours, the car CD-1333 was seen stopping on str. Al. I. Cuza, in front of the Museum of History.

After a minute, out of the car stepped AVRAM VASILE, son of Constantin and Maria, born 01.12.1925, in Hondreni, Suceava county, domiciled in Bucharest; he then entered the Museum of History.

At 16.20 hours, out of the Museum of History came AVRAM VA-SILE, accompanied by two Romanian citizens: the director of the Museum and another clerk at the same institution, who went to the car CD-1333 and, together with the driver of the mentioned car, started taking out of the trunk several pieces of luggage, among which several suit-cases, electronic equipment, American flags, which they carried to the Museum of History.

AVRAM VASILE and the driver of the car CD-1333, named DU-MITRESCU ŞTEFAN, are lodged at "Galaţi" hotel.

Attached, 2 (two) photographs***** and the negative.

Chief of Bureau "F", Lt. Col., ss, BLEOJU NECULAI

A.N.C.S.S.A., *Informative* fund, file no. 1093922, vol. III, ff. 219-222, 239.

Handwritten indication at the beginning of the document: "B.1/H.C.".

* Underlined here and in the rest of the document.

** The seal of the mentioned institution.

*** Rubric left blank.

**** Underlining doubled by a "?" sign.

***** The mentioned photographs were not identified.

-47-

Note by informer "Elly", handed to resident "Cătălin", regarding the visitors of the American Library; diplomat Ernest Latham's activity and moves

311/H.C.	Top Secret
"ELLY"	Unique copy
F.N./0053/04.18.1987	04.20.1987
Received on 04.18.1987	
from "ELLY" by "CĂTĂLIN"	

NOTE

Regarding Romanian visitors to the Library, here is my report:

On April 7, at around 10.45, a citizen came to KIKI; he was approximately 55, thin, tall, wearing glasses, in a beige short coat. *He talked in KIKI's* office* for about 10`.

On April 9, around 13.00 hours, KIKI was visited by the artist PUNEA (ION), GEORGIANA's father, *they talked for about 1h.*

On the same day, around 16.30, PAZDRAL, from the Embassy (U.S.) came to KIKI.

On April 10, at 14.00 hours, KIKI was visited by MIHAI HRISTU, accompanied by a lead singer, for the purpose of a show at the Library.

On the same day, at 16.00 hours, JOHNNY RĂDUCANU also came to KIKI. It is to be noted that, immediately after his arrival, *LATHAM* showed up as well. *They talked for over 1h.*

On April 13, around 10.51, LATHAM came to KIKI, while MIHAI HRISTU was at the Library.

On the same day, at 14.00 hours, the ambassador's wife also came to KIKI.

As usual, LATHAM often visits the Library, many times without talking to anybody. This also occurred on April 17, 8.00 hours, when he walked through the offices, without an obvious reason.

I also mention that on April 8, 09.45 hours, the Soviet cultural attaché came to KIKI.

At the same time, on April 17, 16.30 hours, PAZDRAL, from the Embassy, came again to see KIKI.

Concerning the trip made by BROWNE RICHARD and HEIG to Craiova and Timişoara, I provided information by phone on the route and the persons met on the way. From the talks I had with him, I found he was impressed by the size of the building constructed here, by the different architectural styles and, especially, by the way he was welcomed by Romanian officials.

He did not show any interest for other issues than the subject of the exhibition.

A final meeting before leaving was held on 04.17. 10.00 hours at the Exhibition Offices, in which participated: BROWNE, LATHAM, HEIG, AVRAM, TADISOS (from the Embassy). The Romanian side was represented by CIUHUREZU VICTOR from D.R.E., GEAUȘU VALERIU, director of the Office of Exhibitions, STURZA GHEORGHE and 2 persons from Cinematography.

It was settled for the exhibition to take place in Bucharest at the Sala Dalles, in Craiova at the National Theatre and in Timișoara at the Sports Hall No. 2. The halls in Bucharest and Timișoara which will host movie presentations are to be determined later. Also, the American side is to transmit in due course the list of necessary services to be provided by Office of Exhibitions (workers, machinery, etc.). At the same time, the prospective films to be presented in Romania will be nominated and forwarded in order to be seen and approved.

There was some inconclusive talk about the movies prohibited by the Romanian side for projection in cinemas. N.b., BROWNE is only responsible for the technical aspects of these activities and is to inform the competent authorities on the financial aspects.

***

As for the relations between KIKI and CARMEN, it looks like they have improved, as she will have a lighter work load in the future. In a talk with CARMEN FERARU, she told me that KIKI had said that, before leaving, she will have to draw up a report on each of the Romanian employees describing how they fulfilled their tasks, report to be forwarded to HEIG.

On April 21, LATHAM is to leave for Vienna, to return on 04.25. He will participate in a working session regarding the American grantees to come to Romania.

OLIVIA MARINESCU told me that LATHAM asked her to check if, on the way back from Vienna, he can have a few hours' layover in Budapest, in order to meet a friend, without affecting the total cost of the flight.

Also to be mentioned: KIKI will make a trip to Athens next week.

04.18.1987

"ELLY"

Note

This information was drafted together with the undersigned. I would only want to add that in May, with the exception of the exhibition launch in Brăila (about which I reported in a previous material), an exhibition of books on economy must also be mentioned. Only 60 books arrived, an explanation was requested by telex. If no more books are sent, they will be exhibited without organizing any accompanying reception.

I have discussed with source certain personal issues, which have been bothering him for some time (*his son is involved in an affair with a girl whose parents are fugitives*). She has filed her emigration request, and his son gave up on this "love adventure." Their relationships have improved. Other subjects referred to aspects of the international situation, our country's position, and other issues regarding the social-economic development of our country.

During discussions he demonstrated realism. I understood also from talking to the other Romanian employees that he tries to quiet down certain conflicts and to point them towards reasonable behavior.

This has earned him the esteem of his colleagues and the appreciation of the diplomats, who constantly seek his advice and opinion in professional matters. On Oct. 17, he had a conversation with STROVAS and LATHAM, who could not understand why the Romanian side requires a tax on the rent of halls or on admission tickets to watch certain movies.

"CĂTĂLIN"

N.B.

Information provided by "ELLY" has proved totally accurate. The source has communicated in due course all travels undertaken by HIGHT together with BROWNE.

The note will be exploited in the files regarding the diplomats mentioned in the material.

CPT, ss, HUSZAR

A.N.C.S.S.A., *Intelligence section,* file no. 1093922, vol. III, ff. 242-244.

Handwritten indication at the beginning of the document: "LASCU".

* Underlined here and in the rest of the document.

-48-

Report by D.S.S., based on information from agent "Rică", regarding the activity carried out by diplomat Ernest Latham; Paul Shapiro's arrival in Bucharest

311/H.C.	Top Secret
"RICĂ"	Unique copy
File no. 005558/42	04.26.1987

REPORT

Informer "RICĂ" communicated to us by phone the following:

On 04.25.1987, he went by car to Otopeni Airport, whence he took, at 18.30 hours, LATHAM and another American, both coming from Budapest.

"RICĂ" brought the two to LATHAM's domicile, where the other one stayed for about half an hour (he changed his clothes). Then they came down and LATHAM asked "RICĂ" to take the other foreigner to the "Majestic" hotel.

On the way, the source realized the American citizen knows Romanian well. When they arrived at "Majestic" hotel, the receptionist told the stranger: "Welcome, Mister SHAPIRO", and the foreigner provided no answer, while the source drew the conclusion SHAPIRO was not "happy" he had been recognized by the receptionist.

N.O.

"RICĂ" will continue to keep us informed about the activities which SHAPIRO participates in and the persons he comes into contact with.

PAUL SHAPIRO has visited Romania and the Embassy before, for cultural purposes.

Material will be exploited at ind. 3

11/H.C.

Lt.-maj. ALECU ILIE

A.I./C.S./unique copy/R.D.692/1987

A.N.C.S.S.A., *Intelligence section*, file no. 1093922, vol. III, p. 247.

-49-

Note by informer "Lovinescu" regarding Ernest Latham's visit to his domicile, conversation on the diplomat's doctoral thesis

Source "LOVINESCU"   04.29.1987

361/C.V./04.30.1987 / F.N.

[INFORMATION NOTE]

Yesterday, 04.28.1987, between 18.00 and 22.00, I received at my home Mr. LATHAM, U.S. cultural attaché, to discuss with him about his doctoral thesis (which I received "in installments," with undesirable delays).

Between 18.00 and 20.00 hours, I expounded to him my viewpoints regarding the thesis ("American Writer OLIVER WENDELL HOLMES's View on the Past"), with appreciation for the substance and structure, but also with numerous objections regarding certain details (omissions, "technical mistakes" caused by the "Xerox" copying, some criticisms of substance, the lack of "context" for HOLMES's contribution as background in the anti-Calvinist struggle and the growth of the medical sciences in his period, etc.). I have appreciated that he accepted without reservations most of my objections. As it stands, the work has clear merits and I believe that, in its final form, it will meet the scientific standards of a doctoral thesis in the philological sciences.

We have agreed on the following working stages:

a) By May 10-15, CY I will receive the paginated text (so far I have only had loose pages at my disposal), with the suggested corrections;

b) By then, I will receive the obligatory *abstract** of the thesis (½ in Romanian, ½ in English);

c) I will contact the co-referents to the dissertation (Lect. GEORGETA DUMITRIU, PhD, Lect. SEVER TRIFU, PhD, Lect. DAN GRIGORESCU, PhD). The president of the commission will be Prof. HANȚĂ, the dean of the Faculty of Philology in Bucharest.

There is a certain urgency in solving these issues, as Mr. LATHAM is to leave Romania for good around *July 1, 1987*, in order to take over the position of cultural attaché in Greece (Athens).

Between 20.00 and 22.00 hours, we had a conversation during a Romanian style dinner prepared by my wife; VERONICA FOCȘĂNE-ANU, our daughter, and her own daughter, DANIELA, also took part.

Besides the aspects connected to the dissertation, I have noted:

a) Mr. LATHAM's interest in our folklore (we also talked about his translation of "Miorița", published in the flyer of last year's exhibition at the American Library, an accomplished translation, but... in prose);

b) his regret that his daughter CHARLOTTE, ??** years old, who got used to her Romanian friends, will miss them in Greece;

c) *his interest in the situation of Gypsies in our country*;

d) his good knowledge of our literature;

e) his appreciation for our intellectuals, students, and pupils (plus their capacity to learn foreign languages, more precisely English);

i) his regret that he is not invited for symposia, conferences, school and university events;

j) the fact he is a little late with his work, as he had to leave for Vienna (and he is to leave again for Vienna at the end of this week).

I mention the fact that, unlike last time, Mr. LATHAM drove himself in his own car or that his attention towards his "hosts" manifested itself by the gift of a number of books (novels, detective stories), a bottle of *whisky,* and a box of *Kents,* and ¼ kg coffee.

***

With reference to Comrade TRAIAN FILIP's translation from CĂLINESCU's *History of Romanian Literature*: I received from him and examined another app. 250 pages. I am to receive the remaining 400 pages piecemeal. According to Comrade FILIP's estimation, the English translation of the volume will be published on July 1, 1987.

ss, LEON LEVIȚCHI

Note of the Bureau
Material is exploited, in original, at 311/H.C.
CPT, ss, undecipherable

A.N.C.S.S.A., *Informative* fund, file no. 1093922, vol. III, ff. 248-249.
* Underlined here and in the rest of the document.
** It is the form in the original.

-50-

Report by informer "Ortansa" regarding Ernest Latham's activity; the diplomat's refusal to surrender his passport on buying travel tickets

311/H.C.   Top Secret

"ORTANSA"   Unique copy

05.07.1987

REPORT

In order to buy his travel ticket to Cluj and Iaşi, respectively, for the purpose of accompanying an American reader, invited by the Cultural Section, ERNEST LATHAM was supposed to surrender his passport, which was absolutely indispensable. The diplomat refused to surrender the passport, asking why his diplomat's identity card was not sufficient, as in other instances. It was explained to him that the passport was necessary for official travels, while for personal ones the diplomatic ID was used. LATHAM did not agree to surrender his passport and up to now the tickets have not been purchased.

N.B.

Aspects regarding ERNEST LATHAM will be exploited, in copy, at 311/P.C.

CPT HUSZAR C.

H.C./C.S./unique copy/R.D.792/1987

A.N.C.S.S.A., *Intelligence* group, file no. 1093922, vol. III, p. 254.

-51-

Communication by 3rd Directorate within D.S.S.,
to Bureau III within Sibiu County Inspectorate
of the Ministry of Internal Affairs, regarding
the notification of diplomat Ernest Latham's
unofficial visit to Sibiu; "suspicions he is
carrying out intelligence activities", proceedings for intelligence control

Ministry of Internal Affairs	Top Secret
Department of State Security	Unique copy
3rd Directorate	
No. 311/P.C./D/0015052/05.19.1987	TELEX*

To the Sibiu County Inspectorate of the Ministry of Internal Affairs

For the attention of the Chief of Securitate

This is to inform you that the American diplomat ERNEST LAT-
HAM, cultural attaché of the Embassy, accompanied by his eight years
old daughter, will arrive in Sibiu by airplane on 05.23.1987.

ERNEST LATHAM is on an unofficial visit, to spend his weekend.

Taking into consideration the diplomat is to leave his position for
good and there are suspicions he is carrying out intelligence activities,
please undertake complex intelligence control proceedings on him for
the duration he is within your area of competence.

The resulting materials are to be sent to us in due course, to 311/P.C.

f. Chief of Directorate, Lt. Col., ss, undecipherable*

P.C./C.S./unique copy/R.D.804/1987

A.N.C.S.S.A., *Intelligence* group, file no. 1093922, vol. III, p. 259.

* Undecipherable signature.

-52-

Communication by Major General Aristotel Stamatoiu, adjunct of the Minister of Internal
Affairs, to Lieutenant General Iulian Vlad,
adjunct of the Minister of Internal Affairs,
forwarding a note of MB 0544 regarding diplomat
Ernest Latham's relations with the literary
historian George Muntean and the sociologist
Georgeta Gheorghe

Ministry of Internal Affairs   Top Secret

Department of State Security   Ex. no. 1

Cabinet of the Adjunct of the Ministry of Internal Affairs

No. 0081951 din 05.30.1987

To Comrade Adjunct of the Ministry of Internal Affairs

Lieutenant General IULIAN VLAD

Find the attached material no. 225/0081951 of 05.30.1987 regarding
the cultural attaché of the U.S. Embassy in Bucharest.

Adjunct of the Minister of Internal Affairs

General-lieutenant, ss, ARISTOTEL STAMATOIU

[Annex]

MB 0544   Top Secret

No. 225/0081951 of 05.30.1987   Copy no. 1

NOTE

We have information that the cultural attaché of the U.S. Embassy in Bucharest maintains relationships with GEORGE MUNTEAN, literary historian, whom he also visits at his home, as well as with GEORGETA GHEORGHE, sociologist at the Institute of Design for Standardized Buildings in Bucharest (laboratory of sociological research).

The American diplomat manifests an interest in getting recommendations of Romanian sociologists to be offered research grants in the U.S.A., but these persons have "to be serious", because during the recent period, in his opinion, specialists in this field were sent to his country who "had to carry out intelligence activities".

A.N.C.S.S.A., *Informative* fund, file no. 1093922, vol. III, ff. 267-269.

Resolution: "Comrade General MORTOIU, what does the 3rd Directorate know? Proceedings for control and interdiction. / Lieutenant General, ss, IULIAN VLAD / 06.01.1987".

-53-

Note by Bureau III within Iaşi County Inspectorate of the Ministry of Internal Affairs, to the 3rd Directorate within D.S.S., regarding the visit to Iaşi of Professor Henry Schvey, accompanied by cultural attaché Ernest Latham

Ministry of Internal Affairs	Top Secret
Iaşi County Inspectorate / Securitate – Bureau III	Ex. no. 1
No. 3/B.I./0035718 of 06.03.1987	

To the Ministry of Internal Affairs

Department of State Security / 3rd Directorate – Bureau 1

Bucharest

Following your order no. 311/P.C./D/0015052 of 05.19.1987, regarding the trip undertaken by American cultural attaché LATHAM ERNEST to Iaşi municipality, we report:

On the evening of 05.20.1987, the driver of the U.S. Embassy in Bucharest, OLTEANU CONSTANTIN, arrived in Iaşi on board in an Oldsmobile, registry number CD-1345, and was lodged at the hotel Traian. After dinner, he went to his room without any contact with Romanian or foreign citizens.

On 05.21.1987 there arrived in Iaşi LATHAM ERNEST, cultural attaché at the U.S. Embassy in Bucharest, together with Professor SCHVEY HENRY, and were lodged at the hotel Traian, then had breakfast in the White Hall of the restaurant.

Following the special proceedings undertaken, it is known that SCHVEY HENRY is a professor of English at *Leiden University* (Holland) and has a company of amateur actors, whom he personally trains, and he is concerned about their fate after his return to the U.S., this coming fall.

During talks, LATHAM ERNEST was very laconic, leaving the initiative to SCHVEY HENRY. Meanwhile, the driver OLTEANU C. put into the trunk of the car 4 boxes containing "Sinteza" magazines, which were later delivered to the University. There were five other boxes in the trunk, of different sizes.

After a short walk in the central area, LATHAM E. and SCHVEY H. went to the "Al. I. Cuza" University, where they were welcomed by HOLBAN HORIA and AVĂDANEI ŞTEFAN, in the attention of

Bureau III-Iași, the latter being known [to LATHAM] from his previous visit to Iași. LATHAM ERNEST expressed his regret for not being welcomed also by VEREȘ GRIGORE, Chair of English Language Department (who had left the city for business), he tried to find out if he was in Iași or not.

During SCHVEY HENRY's conference, LATHAM studied very carefully the physiognomies of the persons present, following closely especially their mien and gestures, the way they were looking and discussing, without getting involved in any conversation, while SCHVEY continued after the conference to talk to ODETA CAUFMAN, lecturer at the Chair of English Language, daughter of the chief of the Jewish community in Iași, and a specialist in issues of theatre.

After the end of the conference, the two American citizens stayed at the Chair, and LATHAM E. asked HOLBAN HORIA, AVĂDANEI ȘT. and ALBU RODICA about the American lecturer JERRY McGUIRE, getting the answer that the latter was on a trip to Brașov.

LATHAM ERNEST also enquired if the Romanian side was content with the books sent to the Reading Room, and HOLBAN HORIA, deputy of the Chair, thanked him for the books received, mentioning that they filled up certain voids that had appeared in the last years, when no more books had been sent. LATHAM ERNEST smiled ironically, saying that as far as he knew, there was no Reading Room now and no place to send the books. HOLBAN HORIA retorted that "In Iași, the Reading Room has functioned without interruptions and it is here that the American lecturer came, when he considered it necessary!"

LATHAM E. was asked whether there is an opportunity to borrow books of special interest from the American Library in Bucharest, through the Reading Room, in order to spare those interested of making trips to Bucharest, and the cultural attaché answered this was possible.

OCU OCTAVIA, member of the English Language Department, invited them to her exhibition of sculpture, where they were accompanied by her and AVĂDANEI ȘT., on the way to the National Theatre.

It was ascertained that after the foreigners left for the University, RADU RODICA, from the U.S. Embassy in Bucharest, sent a phone message to the driver OLTEANU C., asking him to go to the lodging of the American lecturer JERRY McGUIRE and to ask him urgently to get in contact with the Embassy, since his phone was not functioning. Investigations showed that JERRY McGUIRE and SUSAN McGUIRE had not been in Iași on that day.

On receiving the message, the driver OLTEANU C. alleged he did not know where JERRY McGUIRE lived, although that was not true.

While they were visiting the painting [sic!] exhibition and LATHAM ERNEST was looking at the exhibits, making favorable remarks, he came closer to lecturer AVĂDANEI ȘTEFAN and cautiously initiated a dialogue with him, out of which the following resulted:

- he is looking forward to the Romanian, whom he appreciates as a specialist in American literature, paying him a visit to Athens, whenever he wishes;

- related to the American lecturer JERRY McGUIRE's absence from Iași for the meeting, E. LATHAM said: "He is not here... I know... I was not expecting him to be... He hates me!"

LATHAM ERNEST added that Iași will continue to receive books for the Reading Room, as now the relationship is fine, asking how things work at the moment. AVĂDANEI ȘT. told him everything was O.K., but from LATHAM's mien it was noticeable he had doubts.

After the dialogue, LATHAM E. approached again Professor SCHVEY, continuing to admire the exhibits.

During the visit to the National Theatre, the participants carried out a specialized dialogue in this field; LATHAM E. carefully studied the physiognomies of the Romanian participants, but did not initiate any discussion with them, only insisting that AVĂDANEI ȘTEFAN should sit next to him at the table, and not opposite, as he intended.

After the talks at the National Theatre ended, LATHAM ERNEST told AVĂDANEI ȘT. that they would see each other again at the show tonight, and he is looking forward to it. AVĂDANEI ȘTEFAN answered him he could not make it, as he had another program, then he took his leave from them.

LATHAM E. and SCHVEY H. visited the exhibition of paintings by the Bucharest artist AUGUSTIN COSTINESCU.

Around 20.15 hours, LATHAM E. and SCHVEY H. had dinner, during which they talked about the attempt they will make to offer a Fulbright grant, to teach in the U.S.A. for 6 months, to lecturer ODETA CAUFMAN, from the English Language Department in Iași, whom SCHVEY considers "brilliant". They both consider that she stands a good chance, "as she is Jewish". CAUFMAN ODETA is knowledgeable at both the theoretical and practical level, and they would have liked to invite her to dinner immediately, but did not do so as they were not in the U.S.A. at the time.

SCHVEY HENRY absolutely wishes to bring ODETA CAUFMAN to the U.S., and he will undertake all steps necessary to this end.

That very same evening, SCHVEY H. had a phone conversation with ODETA CAUFMAN, establishing that they would stay in touch for the purpose of achieving her grant to the U.S. He would be sending her specialty books through the American Library in Bucharest.

On 05.22.1987, in front of Unirea hotel, professor SCHVEY H. met the Bucharest painter AUGUSTIN COSTINESCU, who greeted him, but SCHVEY HENRY looked definitely upset by this.

Around 09.15 hours, LATHAM E. and SCHVEY H. went to the airport, leaving for Bucharest by plane.

On the same morning, at 06.10, the McGUIREs returned to Iași from Brașov and went directly home and to bed. The driver OLTEANU C. paid them a visit around 10.30, and it was subsequently established that the American lecturer JERRY McGUIRE said he was upset by that, making no comment on LATHAM E.

During the secret search carried out in Professor SCHVEY HENRY's room, inside a typewritten book, bound in soft red covers, bearing the title "Snowstorm", a letter in English was found, belonging to AUREL M. BADIN, from Bucharest, a translation of which we attached to the present report, together with 4 sheets and 10 photographs**, representing the result of the "F" proceedings that had been undertaken.

Chief of County Securitate

Colonel, ss, CIURLĂU CONSTANTIN*

Chief of Bureau III, colonel, ss, BOȚÎRLAN MIHAIL

Copy 2/B.I./G.M./R.D.003245/396/06.01.1987

[Annex]***

Top Secret   *Copy*

May 20, 1987

Bucharest

Dear Sir,

I very much wish to bring to your attention the dramas here written and sent by me…

If you like them, I have the pleasure to inform you that a copy, in English and Romanian, may also be secured from Mrs. OTILE MARSH, 5 Caroline Place News London – W.2 – 4 A Q, tel. 01-229-4952.

I am also sending a copy of the drama "Psoriasis", in French and, as I have stressed, I require no money but that a quantity of butter should be sent for the Romanian orphans, through an institution of foreign aid. I heard the Common Market is selling butter to the Russians at 219 dollars per ton. I hope a similar price may be obtained for the Romanian orphans.

Anyway, the Russians are responsible for their own poverty.

Thank you for your kindness.

AUREL M. BADIN

Calea Dorobanţi 228

Buch 71 285 / Telefon (90) 33.65.03

[Annex]

Ministry of Internal Affairs	Top Secret
Insp. Jud. Iaşi – Securitate / Bureau "F"	Unique copy
No. 0076281 of 05.22.1987	

To the Iaşi County Inspectorate of M.I.

Securitate – Bureau III

In answer to your address no. 0035701 of 05.20.1987, we convey:

NOTE REGARDING SURVEILLANCE OF THE NAMED LATHAM ERNEST, WHO WAS GIVEN THE CONSPIRATO-RIAL NAME "LASCU", U.S. DIPLOMAT, LODGED AT "TRAIAN" HOTEL-IAŞI, UNDERTAKEN ON MAY 21 AND 22, 1987

Activity of the Target

On 05.21.1987, 08.50 hours, target "LASCU" was taken under sur-veillance from the moment he arrived by plane at the Iaşi Airport, to-gether with the co-national professor, carrying with them a diplomatic bag and a shoulder bag. Together they went to the car CD-1345, waiting for them in the parking lot and, the driver at the wheel, went medium speed along the highway at the airport, str. Moara de Vânt, Eternitate, Cucu, B-dul Independenţei, and in front of the "Carmen" block they turned, and went along B-dul Independenţei, str. Ştefan Gheorghiu, C.D. Gherea, Ştefan cel Mare, P-ţa Unirii, stopping in front of Traian hotel. Target "LASCU" and his colleague, who received the nickname "LUCA", stepped down, took the luggage they had come with and en-tered the hotel, at 09.10 hours.

At 10.25 hours, "LASCU" and "LUCA" came out of the hotel, "LASCU" having a photo camera on his shoulder, and together, talking, crossed P-ţa Unirii, stopping in front of Al. Ioan Cuza's statue, looked at it for about 5 minutes, then continued along str. Cuza Vodă and stopped in front of the window of the workshop for the manufacture of hats. They looked at the exhibited products for approximately 2 minutes, then con-tinued up to the crossroad with str. 11 iunie, where they stopped, crossed to the other side, and went up to the billboard of the National Theatre, looking at the poster referring to the show "Gala of Actors' Recitals". Then, "LASCU" and "LUCA" continued their walk along str. Cuza Vodă, P-ţa Cuza Vodă, and entered "M. Eminescu" bookstore, at 10.55.

They came out immediately, it could not be noticed that they had bought anything, and, talking, went down strada Cuza Vodă and entered the Art Galleries. They just had a look at a few pictures, next to the entrance, then came out, crossed the Passage Piața Unirii, stopping next to the car. "LASCU" took out of his pocket the magazine "România Pitorească", which he leafed together with the driver, while "LUCA" entered the hotel and came back in about 2 minutes, carrying his shoulder bag. They got into the car and went along strada Arcu, Muzicescu, Calea 23 August, stopping in front of Al. I. Cuza University, Building "A". They stepped out, and were welcomed by AVĂDANEI and HOLBAN, other teaching staff, exchanging polite greetings, then, accompanied by the two, "LASCU" and "LUCA", entered the University and went to the Chair of English Language, at 11.05 hours.

We mention that meanwhile the driver of the CD car took several small format cardboard boxes inside the University, and it was noticed that more such boxes were left in the car.

Between 11.10-11.45, while the target was at the University, the special proceedings by the intelligence authority were carried out at the target's lodging place.

At 13.15 hours, target "LASCU", "LUCA", the named HOLBAN and a woman (about 30 years old, 1.65 m high, blond to reddish hair)****, came out of the University using the door of Building "B" of the Politechnic Institute and, talking among themselves ("LUCA" holding a bunch of tulips), went to the CD car, got in and left along Calea 23 August, P-ța Tineretului, Gh. Dimitrov, B-dul Independenței up to I.M.F., stopping in front of the "Rotonda", where they stepped down and entered the exhibition, led by the woman mentioned above. Inside they visited the painting exhibition of IULIA FRUJINOIU, receiving explanations from the person accompanying them and commenting on the exhibits.

At 13.40 "LASCU", "LUCA" and HOLBAN came out of the place, guided by the woman up to the front, where they took their leave from her (who reentered the exhibition), got into the CD car and went along strada Iosif Cihac, stopping in front of the restaurant "Bolta Rece". "LASCU", "LUCA" and HOLBAN stepped down and entered, while the driver stayed in the car; they visited the wine cellar and the garden, then entered the restaurant, choosing a table in the middle of the place.

We mention that, while they were in the restaurant, there were no other customers.

At 14.10 hours, the named HOLBAN left restaurant "Bolta Rece". At 14.15, "LASCU" and "LUCA" came out of the restaurant, got into the CD car and went along str. Rece, Cihac, Universității, B-dul Independenței, D. Gherea, stopping at the side entrance of the National Theatre, where they got out of the car and entered the building, at 14.20, and the driver stayed in the car.

We mention that at the entrance they were greeted by the director of the Theatre, M.R. IACOBAN.

At 15.40 "LASCU" and "LUCA" left the theatre through the same door, got in the CD car and went along str. D. Gherea, B-dul Ștefan cel Mare, str. Vasile Alecsandri, stopping in the front of the shop "Moldo-Plast". "LASCU" and "LUCA" stepped out and went to the "Consign-ația" shop, looked for about 5 min. at the exhibited merchandise, while the driver left by car.

After leaving the shop, "LASCU" and "LUCA" walked along str. V. Alecsandri, Cuza Vodă, entering "Broderia (Embroidery) Miorița", they stayed inside for about 1 min., then continued to walk down str. Cuza Vodă, D. Gherea, and in front of the Special (Assistance) School on this street *they exchanged greetings with ALBU RODICA*****, from the English Language Department of the University, who was coming from the opposite direction.

Then, after walking a few more meters on the street mentioned above, they stopped and looked at the National Theatre, and "LASCU" took a picture of the edifice with the camera he was carrying, then they walked on up to B-dul Ştefan cel Mare and stopped, and "LASCU" took another picture of the National Theatre building, from the front.

After this, "LASCU" and "LUCA" walked on, talking and looking at the buildings around, until they arrived in front of the bookstore "Casa Cărţii", where they stopped, looked at the church "Three Hierarchs", which "LASCU" photographed, then continued to talk to "LUCA", explaining something to him and pointing to the Palace of Culture and the Metropolitan Church, and after about 5 min. they separated.

After splitting, "LASCU" entered the bookstore "Casa Cărţii", at 16.05, where he visited the book stands, the ones in the department "Books in foreign languages" included and bought several volumes, from "Gifts", for which he paid 301 lei.

After separating, "LUCA" crossed the street and visited the shops "Fluieraşul" and "Olimp" on B-dul Ştefan cel Mare and looked at other shop windows in the area between the crossroads with Max Wexler and "Trei Ierarhi", and at 16.20 he entered "Casa Cărţii", where he met "LASCU".

At 16.30 "LASCU" and "LUCA" left the bookstore and walked along str. C. Negri up to in front of the shop "Moldova", where they stopped and "LASCU" took a picture towards Casei Dosoftei – Palace of Culture, then they entered the mentioned shop, where they bought a bag from the book stand and put the books into it, then they visited the ground floor, and Ist, IInd and IIIrd levels of the shop, without buying anything and without stopping at any department in particular.

At 16.55 they came out of the shop, "LASCU" was carrying the book bag, and went along str. A. Panu, stopping in front of the Palace of Culture, and the target took again a picture of it, went to Ştefan cel Mare's statue, where they stopped and talked among themselves for 10 min., noticing that "LASCU" was doing most of the talking, explaining something to "LUCA", both looking around at the buildings in the area.

Then, "LASCU" and "LUCA" went down B-dul Ştefan cel Mare up to the Metropolitan Church, where they turned and walked to the bookstore Casa Cărţii, where they bought three more books, came out and continued to walk along B-dul Ştefan cel Mare, P-ţa Cuza Vodă, entering the restaurant Select. They had a look inside, then came out and entered the restaurant "Mioriţa", where they took a table and had beer, at 17.25 hours.

At 17.45 hours, they came out of the restaurant, walked through P-ţa Cuza Vodă, str. Cuza Vodă, entering the art gallery Cupola in P-ţa Unirii, at 17.50. They looked at the exhibition of paintings and graphic art by *painter AUGUSTIN COSTINESCU*, and after about 10 min. they started talking to the painter AUGUSTIN COSTINESCU, continuing to look at the paintings together with him, getting explanations as well as a folder on the mentioned exhibition.

While they were talking, another man approached them, approximately 45 years old, of somewhat short height, dark-haired, with a beginning of front and rear baldness, whom COSTINESCU introduced to the target and his companion. After about 5 min., the men left the exhibition and went to an address in strada Armeană no. 1, Bloc L-1, section 1, 3rd floor, apartment 3, an address bearing the name CREŢU MARIA on the calling card.

At 18.35 "LASCU" and "LUCA" left Cupola Gallery, crossed P-ţa Unirii and entered hotel Traian.

At 18.50, "LASCU" and "LUCA" came out of the hotel, and in front of it got into the CD car, and went through P-ţa Unirii, and along B-dul Ştefan cel Mare, str. D. Gherea, stopping in front of the National Theatre. They got out of the car and waited in front of the Theatre until 19.00 hours, when MIRCEA RADU IACOBAN came to them from inside and invited them into the auditorium, where they watched the drama "Epitaph for George Dillon", from the central loge.

At 20.10, "LASCU" and "LUCA" came out of the theatre, before the end of the show, got into the CD car parked in front, the driver waiting inside, and went along str. D. Gherea, B-dul Ştefan cel Mare, P-ţa Unirii, stopping in front of Traian hotel. They got out of the car and remained in front of Traian restaurant, while the driver went inside and came back in about 3 min., had a short exchange and then "LASCU" and "LUCA" took their leave from the driver and entered the restaurant, going to the White Hall, at 20.20 hours.

In the restaurant, they sat at a table and had food and drink, while holding a conversation.

We must mention that at the same time in the White Hall there was a group of foreign tourists, who left at 21.30.

At 22.25, "LASCU" and "LUCA" left the restaurant and went to Hotel Traian.

Up to 22.40 hours, when surveillance was suspended, "LASCU" and "LUCA" did not leave the hotel.

On 05.22.1987, 08.10 hours, the driver of the CD car left the hotel with the luggage, a black shoulder bag, a diplomat suitcase and a plastic bag, which he deposited in the car trunk.

At 08.15 hours, out of the hotel came "LUCA" accompanied by the receptionist and went to Hotel Unirea, entering, and about 3 min. later out came target "LASCU", who went to the driver of the CD car, talked to him for a few minutes, then he also went through P-ţa Unirii to Unirea, and entered it.

After approximately 10 min., the target "LASCU", "LUCA" and the receptionist came out of Unirea, crossed P-ţa Unirii to the front of the Traian hotel next to the car, took leave of the receptionist. Then "LUCA" took a pen out of a coat inside the car trunk and hurriedly entered the hotel.

While "LUCA" was inside the hotel, "LASCU" went to the front of the A.I. Cuza's statue, looking carefully at the entire monument. After about 3 min. "LUCA" came out of the hotel, went to target "LASCU", and together they returned to the CD car, climbed in and left along P-ţa Unirii, B-dul Ştefan cel Mare, Străpungerea Ştefan cel Mare, P-ţa Cuza Vodă, str. V. Alecsandri, B-dul Independenţei, Târgu Cucu, str. Moara de Vânt, continuing their trip to the Iaşi Airport. Here, "LASCU" and "LUCA" stepped out, took the diplomat suitcase and the shoulder bag and entered the airport, where they secured their air tickets.

At 09.25 hours, target "LASCU" and "LUCA" left for Bucharest by plane.

We note the CD car waited at the airport until the plane took off, then the driver left and went along the normal route to the domicile of target "ROLAND", American lecturer, where he parked the car and went inside, at 09.50.

While they were under surveillance in Iaşi Municipality, it was established that target "LASCU" and "LUCA" carried out official activities within Alexandru Ioan Cuza University at the Chair of English Language, at the same time they were concerned with visiting cultural sites: the National Theatre, Casa Cărţii (the House of Books), the Palace of Culture and Casa Dosoftei (Dosoftei House).

Target "LASCU" and "LUCA" also visited the Art Gallery in the Rotonda hall and Cupola, talking with the exhibitors. The targets were accompanied by official persons known to us to be assigned for this work.

Surveillance terminated.

Chief of Bureau, colonel, ss, RUS PETRU

[Annexes]

A.N.C.S.S.A., *Intelligence* section, file no. 1093922, vol. III, ff. 271-281.

* The official stamp of the respective institution.

** Only four photographs were identified and reproduced in the present report.

*** Handwritten indication at the end of the letter: translated from English, / ss, undecipherable. / It was found within the book entitled *Snowstorm*, typewritten and bound in red cardboard".

**** Handwritten indication: "OCU OCTAVIA (lecturer at the Chair of English Language)".

***** Underlined here and in the rest of the document.

****** This caption accompanies each photograph.

Resolution: "B.1 / Studies and proposals".

-54-

Report by the 3rd Directorate within D.S.S. concerning cultural attaché Ernest Latham's relationship with literary historian George Muntean and with sociologist Georgeta Gheorghe;
Latham – specialist in espionage and first
class diplomat, extremely skillful and intelligent"

3rd Directorate	Top Secret
Bureau I	Unique copy
311/P.C.	Date: 06.12.1987

REPORT

Referring to the message sent by MB 0544/225/0081951 / 05.30.1987, we report the following:

The fact is confirmed that ERNEST LATHAM, cultural attaché at the U.S. Embassy in Bucharest, maintains relationships with GEORGE MUNTEAN, literary historian, and with GEORGETA GHEORGHE, sociologist at the Institute of Design for Standardized Buildings in Bucharest.

GEORGE MUNTEAN is in the control of Comrade Col. BANC, from S.M.B. The relations of the American diplomat with GEORGE MUNTEAN are motivated by the fact LATHAM is completing a PhD in our country on a theme of literature and has been, over time, passionate about Romanian culture, even making personal contributions: an accomplished translation of the ballad Miorița, published in the U.S.A. and an introduction to the History of Romanian Literature, by GEORGE CĂLINESCU, the edition issued by IOSIF CONSTANTIN DRĂGAN.

GEORGETA GHEORGHE is under the control of 3rd Dir. (CPT MOCANU) for multiple relationships with foreign diplomats, with persons displaying hostile attitudes and making hostile comments. Her relationship to ERNEST LATHAM has not been relevant, as she was in touch rather with the director of the American Library, MELANIE SKAGEN MUNSHI.

Both ERNEST LATHAM, and MELANIE MUNSHI are leaving the post during this month.

As for the assertion that LATHAM manifests an interest in Romanian sociologists being recommended to him, we can report that the American side is interested to offer research grants to Romanian specialists in several fields of activity. We attach, as an example, a telex received by FRANK STROVAS, counsellor for press and culture.

We also note it is improbable that ERNEST LATHAM may have required introductions to persons who are not *"Securitate's people"**, taking into account *he is an espionage specialist and a first class diplomat, extremely polite and intelligent.*

Of. sp. III, CPT, ss, PĂUN C.

A.N.C.S.S.A., *Intelligence* section, file no. 1093922, vol. III, p. 270.

* Underlined here and in the rest of the document.

Resolution: "06.12.1987 / Communicate to 3rd Dir. and S.M.B. / ss, undecipherable".

-55-

Note by resident "Stan", based on information
from driver Ion Rîpeanu, referring to diplomat
Ernest Latham; source - Latham used to be
"C.I.A. chief for all N.A.T.O. troops in Europe" and "his appointment to Romania was a
sort of vacation"

311/S.I.   Top Secret

"STAN"   Unique copy

House "Perla"   06.27.1987

File no. 002381/00216

NOTE

The source informs:

In a conversation with RÎPEANU ION, the driver of the cultural attaché who resides on Str. Plantelor, he affirmed (while being alone with
the source) the following:

– The above mentioned diplomat was C.I.A. chief for all N.A.T.O.
troops in Europe and his appointment to Romania was a sort of vacation
for him.

On 06.26.1987, he sent by diplomatic pouch from the Embassy 59
very heavy personal boxes. Source has witnessed this diplomat sending
on several occasions very many boxes. The said diplomat, in a dialogue
with the head of the U.S. Embassy's security, KELLY, had a rather
strange behavior (feet up on KELLY's desk, while the latter was stand-
ing).

The said diplomat, after a period he will spend in the U.S.A., will
return to this country and will then leave for Greece, as a military attaché.

We refer to the American diplomat who was a very good friend of the library chief, KIKI.

N.O.

The informer provided this note on the basis of the general training requirement to report aspects of an operative nature about American diplomats.

The person in this case is the American diplomat LATHAM ERNEST, for the attention of 311/P.C., where I also recommend that the note be exploited.

MJR, ss, STAN ILIE

S.I./C.S./unique copy/R.D.1198/1987

A.N.C.S.S.A., *Intelligence* section , file no. 1093922, vol. III, p. 297.
Handwritten indication at the beginning of document: "LASCU".

-56-

Report by 3rd Directorate within D.S.S. to propose closing the dossier of intelligence surveillance on the diplomat Ernest Latham: "a skillful intelligence officer" with advantageous personal qualities, high cultural attributes and very good training for this specific line of work"

3rd Directorate	Top Secret
Bureau 1	Copy no. 1
311/P.C.	January 28, 1988
No. 15052	

I approve,

Lt. Col., ss, undecipherable

REPORT INCLUDING PROPOSALS FOR CLOSING OF THE I.S.D. "LASCU" REGARDING THE AMERICAN DIPLOMAT ERNEST LATHAM JR.

ERNEST LATHAM JR., conspiratorial name "LASCU", born on 08.11.1938, in Massachusetts – U.S.A., arrived in our country on 09.09.1983, as an attaché concerned with cultural issues. He was married to KAREN ELAINE LATHAM (née JOHNSON JAEHNE) and they had a child. Due to domestic misunderstandings, his wife left Romania for good in the year 1984, and the diplomat remained with only his 5 year old daughter.

"LASCU" graduated Dartmouth College in 1960, then became employed by the U.S. Army, as a lieutenant.

In 1966, he was awarded the doctoral degree at Roosevelt University, then was hired by U.S.I.A., as an intern.

After a period of Arabic language training, he was appointed a deputy attaché in Beirut, within the Cultural Section.

From 1970 to 1973, he was an assistant press and culture attaché in Vienna, then he was called back to Washington, where he took classes in the Greek language.

In 1974, he was appointed a cultural attaché in Nicosia, where he worked until 1977, when he was called back to the headquarters.

In 1979, he was sent to the Military Mission in West Berlin, where he stayed until 1983, when he came to take over his position in Bucharest.

During his presence in this position, "LASCU" benefitted from extensive freedom of movement. Even if McBRIDE, the former cultural counsellor, was well-known for harshness in his relations to subordinates, this never prevented the cultural attaché from organizing programs on his own.

At the same time, in order to prolong his stay in Romania, in August 1984, "LASCU" requested and obtained the approval of authorities in our country to stand for his doctor's exam in world literature. The Department of State of the U.S.A. approved the extension of his stay until 1987.

The activities undertaken by him, his behavior and official pursuits, led to the conclusion that "LASCU" is an intelligence officer under diplomatic cover.

Since his arrival in our country, the diplomat came into close friendly relations with Ambassador DAVID FUNDERBURK and WILLIAM EDWARDS, press attaché, employed by C.I.A.

As a result of the informative operational proceedings undertaken, it was ascertained that, through the medium of WILIAM EDWARDS, he came into contact with certain foreign citizens who are in our country on diplomatic mission or other purposes, whom he used in the work of gathering information. In this context, one must note the connections to the Portuguese diplomat GEORGE AMARALL, former officer in his country's army and who had carried out his activity in several African countries.

Starting in 1984, "LASCU" has taken over contact with the African student TSOTSI NORMA. As she had infiltrated into several African embassies in Bucharest and had the opportunity to travel to Mozambique, Angola, Lesotho, and Zaire, the American diplomat used her to collect information on the political groups existing in these countries and their means of action in their liberation struggle.

After his wife left the country, "LASCU" entered a close relationship with KIKI SKAGEN MUNSHI, director of the American Library, together with whom he undertook many trips in the territory. Under these circumstances, they checked in order to ascertain if they were followed. In the year 1985, during a trip to Oradea, they crossed into the Hungarian P.R., where they remained for 12 hours, without a plausible reason.

His special relations to KIKI SKAGEN MUNSHI allowed him both to involve her in solving intelligence tasks, and to use the Library as a meeting place with Romanian citizens who are the focus of the attention of the American Intelligence Service.

Thus, "LASCU" succeeded to establish contacts both with frequent visitors of the Library, and with persons proposed for travel to the U.S. as beneficiaries of grants, professional exchanges, artistic tours, etc. Such was the case of the Romanian citizen "GRIGORE", biologist by profession, who carries out research activity and has access to works important for the Romanian medical sciences. He met several times with "LASCU" within a private framework, on which occasions he was studied and cultivated by the American diplomat. In his approach process, "LASCU" succeeded to induce the Romanian researcher to admit his connections to the Securitate (S.M.B.), after which he arranged a grant in the U.S.A. for him, where action was taken for the purpose of recruiting him.

"LASCU" proved to be a skillful intelligence officer, who knew how to attract and cultivate within his circle Romanian scientific and cultural personalities, whom he tried to exploit at receptions organized at the American Library and at his or other diplomats' residences. He permanently expressed interest in data and information in the social-political and cultural fields, especially tracking the attitude of Romanian intellectuals towards certain laws or party and state decisions; the careers of certain personalities in the domain of culture and media, the situation of the national minorities.

In the activity of collecting information, "LASCU" made an intense use of American lecturers and grantees in our country. They were directly subordinated to him and periodically produced written reports. At the same time, he organized programs for and accompanied in the country a series of American invitees of the Cultural Section. He took advantage of these opportunities to meet and to establish permanent contact with new people, whom he tried to exploit for information.

He manifested a special interest in the Romanian employees of the embassy. In circumstances controlled by us, he asserted that "Romanians are very interested in keeping their jobs, which means money and prestige, in comparison with their fellow citizens. There are Romanians whom we trust thoroughly as well."

In the activity carried out by him, "LASCU" was at an advantage due to his personal qualities, his high cultural level and very good training for this specific area. He mastered the Romanian language well, had vast knowledge in the domain of the culture and history of the Romanian people. All these things allowed him to easily achieve numerous contacts with intellectuals and artists in our country, but, at the same time, have favored our efforts at interposition and infiltration of certain valuable sources. Thanks to an informative network, it was possible to permanently establish the diplomat's intentions and preoccupations, his behavior, the information he was interested in, the subjective and objective factors influencing his orientations. At the same time, efforts at disinformation and influence were carried out, some of them successfully. Thus, following the efforts undertaken, "LASCU" effectively contributed to the promotion of Romanian cultural values, as he translated the ballad "Miorița" into English and published it in an American magazine and wrote the preface to the *History of the Romanian Literature* by G. CĂLINESCU, the IOSIF CONSTANTIN DRĂGAN edition.

At the same time under circumstances controlled by us, "LASCU" carried out himself an action of influence on diplomat KIKI SKAGEN MUNSHI, to whom he presented, in very favorable terms, the values in the history and culture of the Romanian people.

After his appointment as a cultural attaché in Greece, the diplomat expressed his regret for leaving our country and organized for himself a Romanian room in his residence in Athens.

As to the target's personal preoccupations: one should note first his efforts for his daughter to receive a high standard of care and education; as well as, secondly, some strictly commercial considerations. He was frequently known for buying objects from "Consignația" rather for their economic, not aesthetic, value. We are in possession of data that, after leaving this position, he intended to sell these objects for profit through an antiquarian dealer in West Berlin.

Taking into consideration the above report, as well as the fact that in July 1987, the diplomat left our country, going to Athens to fulfil the same function,

WE PROPOSE:

To approve the closing of the dossier of intelligence surveillance regarding ERNEST LATHAM JR., and keeping it in the Securitate files.

The persons who appear as connections have been identified and checked out. The ones who have operational interest to us have been included in our planning.

Specialist officer III

CPT, SIG, PĂUN COSTICĂ

I agree:

Chief of Bureau

Major, SIG, STĂNESCU GABRIEL

P.C./C.S./3 copies/R.D.139/1988

A.N.C.S.S.A., *Intelligence* section, file no. 1093922, vol. III, ff. 313-315.

Postscript

The publication of the *Securitate* file of Ernest Latham is a notable event. It represents a rare case of such a file – of a foreigner, as opposed to those of former or present Romanian citizens – appearing in print. As this collection of documents shows, while Latham's role as the US cultural attaché to Romania between 1983 and 1987 marks him out in body as an outsider, he was, in spirit, an insider, sympathetic to the ambivalences and ambiguities of Romania's past. Latham admits in his introduction, 'serving in the Communist world and in Romania brought particular challenges'. His file reminds the reader of the intrusiveness of the Communist regime into the lives of citizens, be they Romanian or otherwise. It chronicles the measures taken by the *Securitate* to monitor his activities and at the same time, the methods employed to achieve these objectives. A major weapon in the *Securitate's* armory were informers, as the pages from his file demonstrate; they also show that the institutionalization of police control itself made forms of collaboration a legal requirement. The true identity of the informers in Latham's file are known to him, but they become familiar to readers of this file only by their codenames. Their ubiquity explains why the *Securitate* were as much a state of mind for Romanians as well the instrument of totalitarian control.

At a personal level, these documents allow Latham to appeal to the invocation of Robert Burns, 'Oh would some Power the gift give us, to

see ourselves as others see us'. They offer a selective diary of an individual's activities, and in doing so, restore to history experiences that
may otherwise have been overlooked by the subject. To adapt a phrase
of Timothy Garton Ash, what a gift to memory is a *Securitate* file.[1] As
Katherine Verdery has argued, one of the main tasks of the *Securitate*
was to provide "the category of 'enemy', including spies and various
other types of enemies, and to populate it with real people. The files were
a principal means of doing so...."[2] Latham, often alleged in these documents to be a CIA officer, fit the bill.

When reading Latham's file, we become aware of the work-prac-
tices of the *Securitate*, of an extraordinary expenditure of time, money,
and effort. The need for "conspirativity" (*conspirativitate*) required com-
partmentation that kept each officer's activity and his or her informers a
secret both from colleagues as well as from the public. But such com-
partmentation led to duplication of officers' efforts, inefficiency, and often incoherence. In this regard, *conspirativity* was carried to an extreme
by the *Securitate,* compared with the practice of the political police in
other communist regimes in East Central Europe.

It was only through surveillance of an individual that his or her social networks could be uncovered. Reading my own *Securitate* file shows
that the secret police used surveillance as a means of discovering with
whom I came into contact; as a result, some of my friends were "per-
suaded" to become informants. In the case of the most prolific informer

---

[1]Timothy Garton Ash, *The File* (New York: Vintage Books, 1997), p.12.

[2]Katherine Verdery, *Secrets and Truths. Ethnography in the Archive of Romania's Secret Police. The Natalie Zemon Davis Annual Lectures* (Budapest-New York: Central
European University Press, 2014), p.64.

in my file during the early 1970s, the lure of a passport for emigration to West Germany – he was a Saxon from Transylvania – was the inducement. After the revival of a provision of Gheorghiu-Dej, introduced in 1958, and revived under Decree no. 408 of December 1985, failure to report a conversation with a foreign citizen, was deemed a criminal offense, and this measure was used to pressurize persons into informing.[3] Officers were also instructed to appeal to patriotic sentiment as a ploy, but could also use blackmail "in exceptional circumstances"[4] In fact, many informers were trapped in this way when presented with evidence of their own malpractice at work, sexual indiscretion, or former membership in the anti-Semitic Iron Guard. The result was that at the time of the December 1989 revolution, there were, according to Virgil Măgureanu, head of the SRI (the successor to the *Securitate*), approximately 450,000 informers of whom some 130,000 were active.[5]

The intrusiveness of the *Securitate's* surveillance of Latham, the close watch facilitated by the use of local Romanian embassy staff, either drawn from a pool of *Securitate* officers or recruited as informers, is illustrated by numerous documents in this volume. Latham's file places his life in Romania under a bureaucratic microscope, largely stripping it of its existentialist aim and meaning. What is does not adequately convey to the reader is the gentle beguilement by Romania and the Romanians of the cultural attaché, his deep affection for the friends whom he made there, and his understanding of those who have experienced life under

---

[3]See Decretul 408/1985, art. 14.

[4]*Instrucțiunile nr. D-00180/198. Strict* Secret (Bucharest: Ministerul de Interne, 1987), no pagination.

[5]This author's interview with Virgil Măgureanu, 21 September 1991.

dictatorship and of the strategies adopted for survival. This is evident from his driving spirit behind the creation and the mounting of the *Miorița* exhibition in April 1986, and it is that understanding that continues to drive his support for the creation of an environment in which Romanians are stimulated to place the interest of the country before those of a narrow, personal one.

Dennis Deletant
Visiting 'Ion Rațiu' Professor of Romanian Studies
Georgetown University, Washington, D.C.

Photos

The Embassy of the United States in Bucharest

Ernest H. Latham, Jr. with Ambassador David Funderburk

Ernest H. Latham (center), with Ambassador Roger Kirk (right)
and Romanian scholar George Muntean (left), at the
opening of the Miorita exhibit, April 7, 1986

Ernest H. Latham, Jr. with Melanie "Kiki" Munshi,
head of the American Library in Bucharest

Securitate surveillance photos taken during a trip to Ploisti in 1983

Poster from the Miorita exhibit organized by
the American Embassy and Cultural
Attache, Ernest H. Latham, Jr.

Abbreviations

A.N.C.S.S.A. – Archive of the National Council for the Study of the Securitate Archives

A.D.I.R.I. – Association of International Law and International Relations

A.R.I.A. – Romanian Agency of Artistic Management

A.S.E. – Academy of Economic Sciences

Buch. – Bucharest

C.C. – Central Committee

C.C.E.S. – Council of Culture and Socialist Education/Committee of Culture and Socialist Education

C.D. – Diplomatic Corpse

C.E.C. – Casa de Economii şi Consemnaţiuni, House of Economies and Deposits

C.I.A. – Central Intelligence Agency

C.J.C.E.S. – County Committee of Culture and Socialist Education

col. – colonel

CPT – captain

c.y. – current year

D.R.E. – Department of Foreign Relations

D.S.S. – Department of State Security

I.S.D.– information surveillance dossier

I.D.B.T. – intercepting discussions by means of battery fed transmitters

I.M.F. – Institute of Medicine and Pharmacy

I.N.F. – Intermediate-Range Nuclear Forces

ind. – indicative

MFN – Most Favored Nation

M.I. – Ministry of Internal Affairs

mat. – material

N.L. – Note by Lazăr (officer of Securitate)

n.n. – our note

N.O. – Note of the Officer

no. – number

P.C.R. – Romanian Communist Party

C.P.S.U. – Communist Party of the Soviet Union

G.D.R.– German Democratic Republic

F.R.G. – Federal Republic of Germany

R.S.R. – Socialist Republic of Romania

S.M.B. – Securitate of Bucharest Municipality

S.U.A./U.S.A. – Statele Unite ale Americii/United States of America

Sec. – Securitatea, security

T.O. – technical-operative, operative technique

T.V. – television

tov. – comrade

U.T.C. – Union of Communist Youth